Die Schulung der Sprechfertigkeit im modernen Englischunterricht

Eines der wesentlichen Ziele eines modernen, anwendungsorientierten und schülerzentrierten Englischunterrichts ist, wie in allen gültigen Lehrplänen, Bildungsstandards und Rahmenrichtlinien festgelegt, eine fremdsprachliche Kommunikationsfähigkeit, die zum Abitur hin zu einer differenzierten und diskursiven mündlichen Fähigkeit ausgebaut wird. Damit erweist sich der Englischunterricht einmal mehr als sehr realitätsnah, denn statistische Erhebungen haben gezeigt, dass bei einer Wiederbegegnung mit der englischen Sprache im nichtschulischen Kontext etwa 80 bis 90 % der Kommunikation mündlich erfolgt.

Das vorliegende Heft aus der Reihe *Teaching Skills* macht ein doppeltes Angebot:

- Die folgenden Einleitungsseiten geben einen praxisbezogenen Überblick über die Fertigkeit *Speaking*. Neben grundsätzlichen Überlegungen zu den Zielen und den methodischen Anforderungen an die systematische Schulung der Kompetenz werden Aufgabenformate und ihre Verwendung in den Übungen erläutert.
- Die daran anschließenden Kopiervorlagen (KV) lassen sich flexibel im Unterricht einsetzen. Mit Hilfe dieser Arbeitsblätter können die Schülerinnen und Schüler (S) Teilfertigkeiten üben und damit ihre *speaking skills* insgesamt verbessern. Einleitende Passagen nehmen nochmals Begriffsklärungen vor oder erläutern die Einordnung der jeweiligen Subskill in den Gesamtzusammenhang. Weitere begleitende Texte geben Hilfen und Hinweise und unterstützen so die Lernenden.

So strebt das Heft zweierlei an. Zum einen will es die Unterrichtenden beim oberstufengerechten Vermitteln der Kompetenz *Speaking* unterstützen und ihre *TEACHING skills* stärken. Zum anderen möchte es dazu beitragen, die sprachliche Kompetenz der Lernenden zu verbessern und damit auch deren Chance, in Prüfungssituationen zu bestehen, in denen sie diese Kompetenz beweisen sollen: *teaching SKILLS*.
Die Kopiervorlagen des Heftes sind dabei thematisch geordnet in Formen des monologischen Sprechens (KV 1–KV 5) und des dialogischen Sprechens (KV 6–KV 15), wobei Teilfertigkeiten sich in der Regel von einfacheren zu komplexeren Formen aufbauen. Aber auch andere Teilaspekte wie z. B. die Kontaktaufnahme mit dem Publikum beim monologischen Sprechen werden integriert. Den Abschluss bilden allgemeine Gesichtspunkte wie Fragen der Höflichkeit, interkulturelle Bezüge und Prüfungssituationen (KV 16–19). Jede Kopiervorlage kann einzeln bearbeitet, mehrere oder alle Kopiervorlagen können im Zusammenhang eines kleineren oder auch umfangreicheren Lehrgangs eingesetzt werden.

Strukturelle Voraussetzungen, Sprechmotivation und Sprechfähigkeit

Um die erworbenen kommunikativen Fähigkeiten zielführend und effektiv einzusetzen, wird im Englischunterricht von Anfang an großes Augenmerk auf die Mündlichkeit gelegt. Dialoge werden gesprochen, gemeinsam erarbeitet und präsentiert, Arbeitsergebnisse, Schülervorträge und Präsentationen mit wachsender Komplexität und in immer größerer Freiheit der Rede vorgestellt, zunehmend differenzierte Themen in der Fremdsprache miteinander besprochen und diskutiert usw. Prüfungsformate für den mittleren Bildungsabschluss, aber auch für die Sekundarstufe II und das Abitur tragen diesem Ziel ebenfalls Rechnung. Mehr und mehr hält die mündliche Prüfung im Sinne einer tatsächlichen Kommunikationsprüfung Einzug. Dabei bewegt sich der laut Gemeinsamem Europäischen Referenzrahmen formulierte Anspruch an das Sprachniveau im Bereich der Sekundarstufe II auf der Ebene B2/C1. In einigen Bundesländern ist es auch möglich, Klassenarbeiten und Klausuren in Form einer mündlichen Kommunikationsprüfung durchzuführen, sodass sich ein gewisser Backwash-Effekt für den Unterricht ergibt, der zu verstärkter Integration des Sprechens in den täglichen Unterricht führt.

Im Gegensatz zu diesem strukturellen Wandel ist der Redeanteil von S in den tatsächlich stattfindenden Unterrichtsstunden jedoch noch immer relativ gering und bewegt sich häufig im Bereich von Schweigen bis hin zu maximal einer Minute. Dementsprechend klein ist der Übungseffekt aus dem tatsächlichen Unterricht, und der Lehrer verbleibt mit dem Gefühl, im Hinblick auf etwaige Abschlussprüfungen von Neuem beginnen zu müssen und nicht aus dem vermeintlich Vollen schöpfen zu können.
Aufgabe der Unterrichtsplanung muss es also sein, kreative und anregende Sprechanlässe zu integrieren, die die S herausfordern, ihre Ein- und Ansichten zu bestimmten Themen zu formulieren und über diese Äußerungen ihre generelle mündliche Kompetenz zu profilieren. Soweit dies extrinsisch möglich ist, muss die Motivation der S erhöht werden, sich mündlich zu beteiligen. Darüber hinaus müssen die S Methoden und damit Werkzeuge kennenlernen, die es ihnen erleichtern, sich zu beteiligen oder ihre Redeanteile zu erhöhen. Das setzt voraus, dass die S mit zunehmendem Lernalter auch theoretisches Wissen über die Gestaltung und den Aufbau monologischen und dialogischen Sprechens (→ KV 12 *Speech acts in communication*) erwerben und sich die konkreten Redemittel aneignen, um fachliche und kommunikative Inhalte sprachlich und kulturell adäquat (→ KV 16 *Politeness in conversations*) ausdrücken zu können.
Ein möglicher Weg zur Erhöhung der eher intrinsischen Motivation liegt in der (weitestgehenden) Beachtung des natürlichen Wesens echter Kommunikation, die ihren „Sitz im Leben" hat. Sie setzt voraus, dass bei Aufgabenstellungen auch außersprachliche Einflussfaktoren einbezogen werden, wie z. B. der Sprech- oder Redeanlass, die beteiligten Personen und deren Verhältnis untereinander, nicht-verbale Signale wie Gestik, Mimik oder mitschwingende Emotionen. S fühlen sich dann geneigt, sich auch mündlich einzubringen und das durchaus vorhandene Sprachwissen einzusetzen, um zu kommunizieren, wenn das Thema sie (emotional) anspricht oder (intellektuell) provoziert, wenn ihnen die Situation, in der die Kommunikation stattfindet, entweder ohnehin bekannt oder in ihren Regeln vertraut ist oder von ihnen relativ leicht entschlüsselt werden kann.

Speaking und kooperative Lernformen

Die im Unterricht integrierten Übungsformen auf dem Weg zu einer solchen komplexen kommunikativen Kompetenz sollten deshalb auf die Möglichkeiten der kooperativen Lern- und Kommunikationsformen zurückgreifen. Diese erhöhen ganz automatisch den Redeanteil jedes/r S, ohne den Spaß an Kommunikation und Austausch zu vernachlässigen. Sie sind stets interaktiv angelegt, legen dabei aber die Kontrolle für das Stattfinden und die inhaltliche Tragfähigkeit von fremdsprachlichem Austausch nicht aus der Hand. Solche Formen, die besonders für den kommunikativ orientierten Englischunterricht nutzbar gemacht werden können, liegen z. B. mit dem Blitzlicht, der *buzz group*, den sogenannten *cue dialogues*, dem *discussion ticket*, dem *double circle* oder der *fishbowl* vor. Darüber hinaus ermöglichen kommunikative Lern- und Arbeitsformen auch eine differenzierende Vorgehensweise. Innerhalb der verschiedenen Möglichkeiten müssen sich alle S einbringen (das liegt in der Struktur der kooperativen Lernformen und deren inhärenter Überprüfung bedingt), sie können sich aber auch mit ihrer je eigenen Kompetenz integrieren und auf die Hilfe und Mitarbeit ihrer Mitschülerinnen und Mitschüler vertrauen.

Spiralcurricularer Auf- und Ausbau der Sprechfertigkeit

Im Rahmen der Entwicklung der Skills im Englischunterricht muss auch der Entwicklung der mündlichen Kommunikationsfähigkeit Rechnung getragen werden, indem sie spiralcurricular von einfachen Formen (*making polite conversation / small talk*) zu komplexen Formen (*discussion*, *role play*, *interview*) ausgebaut wird. Dies gilt ebenso für die Formen monologischer Präsentation, die vom Reagieren auf einfache Sprechimpulse (→ KV 1 *Dealing with prompts*) hin zu zunehmend komplexen Präsentationen wie bei der spontanen Auslegung und Deutung einer schwierigen Statistik oder einer zu haltenden Rede (→ KV 4 *Delivering a speech*) entwickelt werden können. Damit verändert sich die Kommunikationskultur der S auch von sogenannter *basic communication* (die eher prozessorientierten Charakter hat) hin zu u.a. produktorientierten Kommunikationsformen wie *(panel) discussion*, *role*

play, *debate* und *interview*, die ein konkretes Ziel haben, das in einem Ergebnis, einer Überzeugungsleistung, einem gefundenen Kompromiss, dem Gewinn eines Wettbewerbes oder dem Erwerb eines Ausbildungsplatzes bestehen kann.
Durch einen sich entwickelnden Lehrgang zur Schulung der Mündlichkeit erwerben die S über die rhetorischen Fähigkeiten hinaus einen wachsenden Einblick in die für die jeweilige Dialogsituation angemessenen Ausdrucksformen sowie die adäquate Stil- und Registerebene. Die S erfassen über die Entschlüsselung der situativen Einbettung und der verwendeten Arbeitsanweisungen, welche Sprechakte, Reaktionen, Sprachformen und welcher Wortschatz von ihnen erwartet werden. Sie lernen zu unterscheiden, ob es sich eher um einen *informal talk* oder eine *official discussion or conversation* handelt, ob die Kommunikationspartner auf verschiedenen Ebenen agieren (Asymmetrie zwischen den beteiligten Gesprächspartnern) oder ob es sich um ein Gespräch unter *peers* handelt und sie passen ihre Äußerungen entsprechend an – eine Fähigkeit, die äußerst lebenspraktische Auswirkungen für sie haben kann.

Aufgabenstellungen und Prüfungsformate

In der Schule wird es entgegen der Idealvorstellung gerade in der Prüfungssituation nicht immer möglich sein, hochmotivierende Fragestellungen oder humorvolle Gesprächssituationen zu generieren, die die S zu einer lebensnahen Kommunikation herausfordern, da das unterrichtliche Umfeld stets präsent bleibt. Jedoch bereits durch die klare Strukturierung eines mündlichen Prüfungs- oder Übungsformates, das für die S transparent und nachahmbar ist, erlangt die Gesprächssituation eine Verbindlichkeit, die Äußerungen hervorbringt. Wenn darüber hinaus eine situative Einbettung erfolgt, die an die Lebens- und Erfahrungswelt der S anknüpft, kann für diese sogar die Prüfung zu einer „echten" Gesprächssituation werden. Ein Bezug zur Lebenswelt der S lässt sich z. B. daran festmachen, dass an ihrer Schule ein (Umwelt-, Kunst-, Sozial-, Austausch-) Projekt zu diesem Thema stattfindet, ihre Rede zum Abitur geschrieben wird, es um ihr Schulgebäude oder die Maßnahmen zum Jugendschutz in ihrer Stadt geht usw. Die Gestaltung und Führung des Gesprächs hat also einen konkreten, nachvollziehbaren Anlass und richtet sich darüber hinaus auf ein konkretes Ziel. Damit wird der freie Dialog neben seiner prozessorientierten Entwicklung zu einem produktorientierten Gespräch, dessen Ergebnisse auch für den Lehrer oder ggf. die Mitschülerinnen und Mitschüler leichter evaluierbar und bewertbar sind.
Eine besondere Form der Herausforderung stellen für die S im Überprüfungszusammenhang selbst bei hohem Kommunikationspotential die Formate des *debating* und *role play* dar. In beiden Fällen müssen die S sich schnell in eine Rolle oder Perspektive eindenken, die ihrer eigenen unter Umständen wenig oder gar nicht entspricht, und diese in einer Auseinandersetzung überzeugend und u.U. auch darstellerisch vertreten. Dies erfordert von ihnen über die sprachlichen Fähigkeiten hinaus ein hohes Maß an Abstrahierungsvermögen und Kreativität. Manche S genießen es jedoch auch, eine andere Identität annehmen zu können und diese mit Leben und Sprache zu erfüllen. Generell sollten diese Überlegungen bei der schülerangemessenen Formulierung von Überprüfungs- und Aufgabenformaten einbezogen werden.

Mündlichkeit und Bewertung

In mündlichen Kommunikationssituationen müssen jedoch generell andere Ansprüche an die Korrektheit und inhaltliche Erfüllung gestellt werden als in der schriftlichen Überprüfung, zumal dies die einzige Testsituation darstellt, die in Echtzeit ablaufen muss. Wie bei der Überprüfung und Beurteilung der Diskurs- und Interaktionsfähigkeit üblich, darf dabei der inhaltliche Aspekt nicht unmittelbar im Vordergrund stehen. Wichtiger als die inhaltliche Erfüllung ist bei dieser Art von Aufgabe stets der Nachweis von Aspekten wie *flexibility*, *turn-taking strategies*, *sociolinguistic competence* u.a., die sich vorwiegend auf Gesprächs- und Interaktionsstrategien beziehen, sowie natürlich der Nachweis der Kernaspekte der mündlichen Kommunikation wie *fluency*, *pronunciation*, *adequacy of vocabulary*, *grammar and style* (→ KV 16 *Politeness in conversations*, KV 17 *Spoken language – everyday English*). Diesen besonderen Charakteristika muss Rechnung getragen werden,

und gerade bei der Bewertung muss man als Lehrer lernen, dass nonverbale Kommunikation und nicht sprachlich kodierte Zeichen des Verstehens und Nichtverstehens ihre Berechtigung haben, dass Füllwörter und wiederkehrende feststehende Formulierungen zur Anwendung kommen, dass es kurze Pausen und unvollständige Sätze geben kann und dass all dies der Qualität der Kommunikation keinen Abbruch tun muss. Mögliche Lösungen und die Beurteilung des Erfüllungsgrades orientieren sich demgemäß an der gelungenen Interaktion, dem sogenannten *discourse management* und der sprachlichen Richtigkeit bezogen auf die Mündlichkeit (d. h. Vorhandensein von bestimmten Sprachfunktionen wie Widerspruch, Bestätigung und Nachfrage bis hin zu Redundanz und Pausen usw.). Darüber hinaus spielen auch interkulturelle Aspekte eine Rolle.
Im Idealfall entstehen Kriterien und Matrices zur Bewertung von mündlicher Kommunikation gemeinsam oder in Abstimmung mit den S, die durch die Übereinstimmung von Fremd- und Selbsteinschätzung auch einen Zugewinn für die Gestaltung weiterer Monologe und Dialoge erhalten. Die Bewertung erfolgt dabei im Wesentlichen nicht holistisch, wendet also nicht *eine* Bewertungsskala für alle Teilleistungen an, sondern legt eine analytische Skala aus mehreren Unterskalen zugrunde, die für jeden einzelnen Bereich mehr oder minder detaillierte Beschreibungen auf verschiedenen Erfüllungsstufen zur Verfügung stellen (z. B. inhaltliche Bewältigung, Interaktionsfähigkeit, Sprachgebrauch, kommunikative Reichweite – vgl. die sächsische Matrix zur Beurteilung der sogenannten sprach- oder fachpraktischen Prüfung; → KV 18 *Evaluating speaking*).

Monologisches und dialogisches Sprechen

Bei der Fähigkeit des *speaking* muss grundsätzlich – wie es auch der Gemeinsame Europäische Referenzrahmen tut – differenziert werden zwischen der Teilnahme an Gesprächen und dem zusammenhängenden Sprechen, also zwischen monologischen und dialogischen Formaten (→ vgl. KV 1–5 *Monologues*, KV 6–10 *Making polite conversation*, KV 11–15 *Interacting more formally*). Diese Formate unterscheiden sich sowohl in inhaltlicher als auch in stilistischer Hinsicht, da zum Teil stark voneinander abweichende kommunikative Akte stattfinden.

Monologisch	**Dialogisch**
• Reaktion auf *prompts* wie Illustrationen (Cartoons, Fotos, Gemälde, Grafiken), Zitate, Statistiken oder kurze Texte • Formen der monologischen Präsentation	• *discussion* • *role play* • *panel discussion* • *interview*
(→ hier auch inhaltliches Vokabular zur Bewältigung der Beschreibungs-/Interpretations-erfordernisse)	(→ hier vorwiegend allgemeiner Wortschatz und Wortschatz zu Erfüllung der verschiedenen Sprechakte und Rollen)

Bezüglich des Reagierens auf verschiedene Arten von Impulsen müssen die S im Laufe des Aufbaus ihrer *speaking skills* auch inhaltlich motiviertes Vokabular zur Beschreibung der verschiedenen *prompts* und ihrer Aussagen erwerben. Darüber hinaus ist beim monologischen Sprechen eine höhere Kohärenz zu erwarten, die zum einen durch sprachliche Mittel hergestellt werden muss, zum anderen daher rührt, dass die Verantwortung für die Entwicklungsrichtung des Monologs beim Sprecher selbst liegt und er/sie sie offensiv beeinflussen kann. Gleichzeitig bedeutet das, dass im monologischen Sprechen eine größere sprachliche Korrektheit erwartet werden darf.
Bei den dialogischen Formen kommt es in noch weit höherem Maße auf metakommunikativen Wortschatz an, mit dem die S die Sprechakte, die eine jede Kommunikation konstituieren, versprachlichen können. Deshalb müssen in Gesprächen, ganz besonders wenn sie von den S sogar die Fähigkeit des Rollenspiels einfordern, typische Merkmale eines Diskurses verwendet werden, wie z. B. *pragmatic conventions*, *fillers*, *grammatical features of spoken language*, *ellipsis*, *repetitions* und so weiter. Die Besonderheiten beider Formen müssen beim Üben, aber besonders in der Beurteilung eine große Rolle spielen.

Für daraus abgeleitete Übungs- und Prüfungsformate bedeutet dies, dass folgende Formate möglich sind, z.T. sogar bereits in staatlichen Prüfungen praktiziert werden. Wichtig bei der Unterscheidung der verschiedenen Formate ist auch hinsichtlich der vorhergehenden Übungsphasen die Frage, ob die S Gelegenheit zur Vorbereitung erhalten oder die Präsentation bzw. Kommunikation mehr oder minder spontan (maximal nach einer kurzen Einlesezeit) erfolgen muss.

speaker(s)	possible formats
monologue situation	independent: presentation on a certain topic (prepared or spontaneous)
	guided: answering questions or reacting to a text
dialogue situation	communicating with a teacher or exam panel
	communicating with one or more equal partners (classmates, applicants …)

Erwerb von Redemitteln

Über den angedeuteten Lehrgang spätestens von Klassenstufe 10 bis 12 bzw. 13 erweitern die S nicht nur ihre Fähigkeiten zur Entschlüsselung der Situation, der Reaktion auf verschiedene Impulse usw., sondern legen konkret ein nach oben offenes, entweder mündliches oder tatsächlich schriftliches Verzeichnis thematisch und situativ geordneter Redemittel an, das sich nach und nach differenziert und erweitert und das sich nicht an Inhalten orientiert, sondern sich den verschiedenen Sprechakten zuordnet. Die S müssen „gezwungen" werden, dieses Verzeichnis systematisch zu erweitern und weitgehend zu automatisieren, denn nur über eine variable Vielfalt solcher kommunikativer Versatzstücke können sie im Idealfall das stilistische Niveau ihres Gesprächs steuern und angemessen auf das Umfeld und die Situation reagieren. Für das vorliegende Heft bedeutet dies, dass die S ein bereits begonnenes Grundrepertoire mündlicher oder schriftlicher Art über das Üben anhand der verschiedenen Kopiervorlagen schrittweise erweitern hin zu einem flexibel einsetzbaren, differenzierten Register, das es ihnen ermöglicht, auf verschiedenste Impulse zu reagieren.
(→ KV 12, die eine Liste an Formulierungen enthält, die die Basis einer schülereigenen Sammlung darstellen könnte).

Speaking und Operatoren

Das Niveau sowie die Verortung des Gesprächs werden in Prüfungssituationen durch die Art der Aufgabenstellung gelenkt, die erstens die situative Einbettung des Gespräches bietet und zweitens über die Operatoren (→ KV 19) das sprachlich-stilistische Register und die Herangehensweise an die Problemstellung steuert. Für die S ist es deshalb ebenfalls wichtig, dass sie über gesichertes Wissen hinsichtlich von Sprache und Register sowie hinsichtlich der Bedeutung der Operatoren verfügen – Wissen, das sie spontan und damit fast intuitiv und ohne Zeitverzug abrufen können. Verlangt die Aufgabenstellung zu beschreiben, zu kommentieren, zu überzeugen, eine Rangliste zu erstellen, zu einem Kompromiss zu finden o.Ä.? So kann auch dem stets gegenwärtigen Vorwurf entgegengewirkt werden, es gehe bei mündlichem Sprechen vorwiegend darum, zeitliche Intervalle mit möglichst vielen Worten zu füllen und eine inhaltliche Bewertung werde zugunsten eines Sprechens um des Sprechens willen bewusst zurückgedrängt. Operatorengestützte Aufgabenformate fordern durch die Festlegung der Art der Auseinandersetzung mit dem Thema automatisch ein bestimmtes Gesprächsniveau ein, das auch ein bestimmtes Register mit sich bringen muss, um eine erfolgreiche Kommunikation oder mündliche Präsentation zu gewährleisten.

Mündliche Mediation und *debating*

Etliche der einschlägigen Hinweise zur Durchführung von Prüfungen in der Sekundarstufe II und im Abitur sehen neben den o.a. Formen des Monologs und des interaktiven Sprechens noch die Kategorie der mündlichen Mediation (→ KV 5) vor, die wie das *debating* (→ KV 14) eine spezifische Sonderform des mündlichen Sprechens darstellt. Bei ersterer kommt zum Akt des freien monologischen Sprechens auf einen bestimmten Input hin die Leistung hinzu, von konkreten Details zu abstrahieren, ebenso die Transferleistung in die andere Sprache. Das *debating* lenkt den Gruppendiskussionsprozess durch ein stark strukturiertes und reglementiertes Format, das zudem von den Diskutierenden verlangt, ggf. von ihrer eigenen Position abzurücken und die Gegenposition überzeugend zu vertreten. Bei beiden Formaten kommen eine Vielzahl von Strategien zur Anwendung, die für das *speaking* im Allgemeinen von Bedeutung sind, darüber hinaus verlangen aber beide eine sichere Kenntnis der besonderen, jeweils spezifischen Regelhaftigkeit dieser Kommunikationssituationen, die in den jeweiligen Kopiervorlagen im Vordergrund stehen soll.

Dr. Annette Leithner-Brauns

Different prompts
Many of your monologues or little presentations will have to be spontaneous. You will have to react more or less immediately to certain cues or prompts, i.e. to
- short texts, e.g. quotations,
- statistics or diagrams,
- visuals like pictures, photos, cartoons or maps,
- short listening texts.

For the different impulses it is necessary to accumulate a range of vocabulary to describe, analyse or even interpret them quickly and appropriately.
Always begin by describing the given material in a structured way. Then move on to the task as stated in the instructions (see operator if it is a test situation).

1 Quotations

Choose one or two of the following quotations and comment on it/them. Look at the box below for language help.

Youth is easily deceived because it is quick to hope. (Aristotle)
The duty of youth is to challenge corruption. (Kurt Cobain)
If youth knew; if age could. (Sigmund Freud)
Youth has no age. (Pablo Picasso)
Youth is wasted on the young. (George Bernard Shaw)

Dealing with quotations
If the prompt is a quotation you should first give information about it, then read it out and finally comment on it.

I was given a quotation by ... • X/Y was/is a ... • Let me read it out to you. • From my point of view it means … • It can be seen as ... • This is true to a certain extent ... • I totally disagree ... • I think it is meant to be ironic ... • On the contrary ... • X/Y expresses a totally opposing view …

2 Statistics or diagrams

Comment on the following charts. You will find some language help at the end of the task.

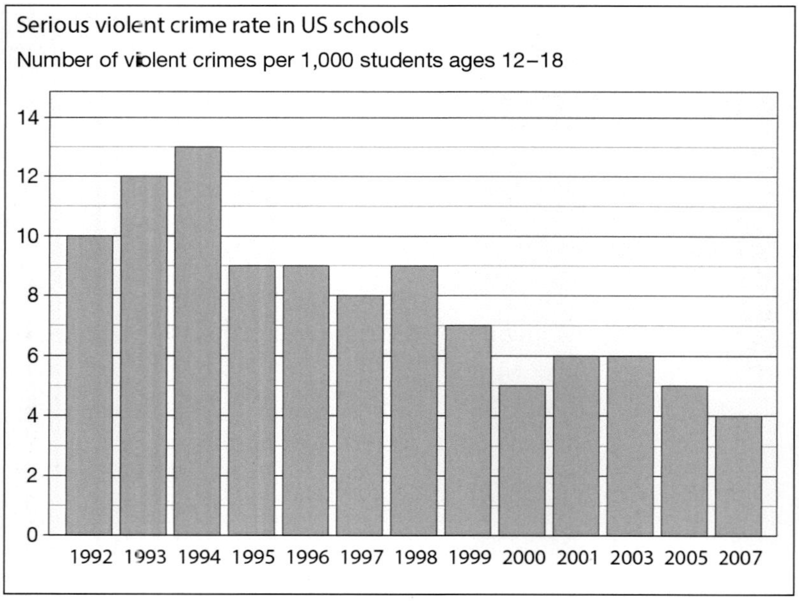

Source: *Virginia Youth Violence Project, University of Virginia*

When dealing with graphs and charts or statistics and diagrams it is important that you analyse them carefully and make sure that you understand the condensed information. Then you identify the type of statistics or diagram that is being used: line graph, bar chart, pie chart, flow chart or table. After that you comment on important aspects, trends, surprising facts etc., but not on every detail. **Line graphs** are often used to present trends (mostly in relation to time). **Bar charts** (horizontal or vertical) mostly compare two or more items. **Pie charts** are probably the most frequently used charts and show the percentage (usually out of 100%) that something (a sector) has of the whole.

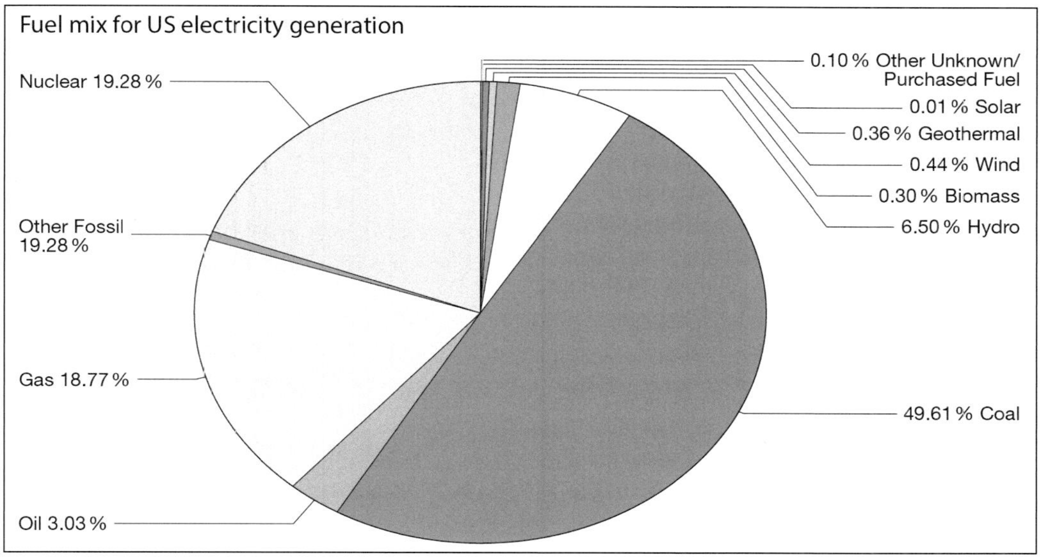

Source: *U.S. EPA, eGRID, year 2005 data*

I was given a bar/pie/flow chart/table. • It shows / it is about ... • on the horizontal axis/vertical axis • the slices/sectors describe ... • There is a growing number of ... • percentage/amount/ number • reached an ultimate peak/low • falling/rising steadily/dramatically/abruptly • decrease/increase • majority/minority of ...

3 Visuals

Comment on the cartoon. You will find some language help in the box below. Don't forget to use the present progressive wherever necessary.

Dealing with visuals
There are different forms of visuals: photographs, symbols or printed images, as well as cartoons. You need to have a fairly broad vocabulary to describe each form when asked for a presentation. It is also helpful to use a certain structure when describing a visual: either from left to right (or the other way round) or from the foreground to the background.

in the picture/photo/ cartoon/drawing you can see • it depicts ... • on the right/left/in the centre • in the foreground/ middleground/ background • the central figure is waiting/eating/ • pointing/... • the picture reminds me of • it is very romantic/ironic/dramatic • it alludes to ... • I think it suggests ...

4 More practice

a) Take something – any random object – out of your bag or ask your partner to do it. (Alternatively, your teacher may give you something.) 'Sell' this object to your class or group, explaining its quality of form and function and why it is the one thing they have always been waiting for. Be persuasive, perhaps funny.

b) Compose sentences, using either the present tense or the present perfect, to put the phrases/sentences below in context by describing a situation in which they could occur.

- Ah, there it is! Pity – it's too late now.
- Never mind, don't worry.
- Do what you have to do, but I don't think it's a good idea.
- Congratulations!
- It's awful – I'm not going to pay for that!
- Great, thanks!
- I can't, it's too late for that, after what Margaret has done.
- Never in my life!

c) Choose one of the following prompts, take notes and comment on it in a two-minute presentation.

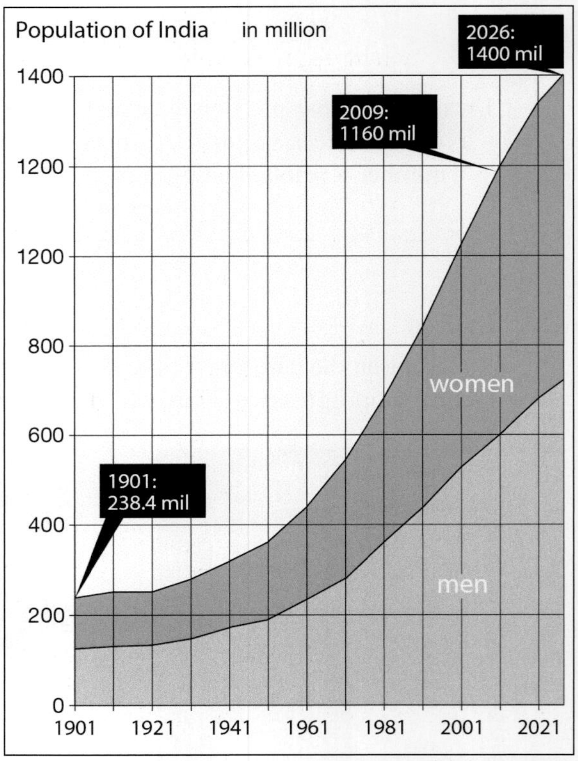

Source: Census of India

'India is the cradle of the human race, the birthplace of human speech, the mother of history, the grandmother of legend, and the great grand mother of tradition. Our most valuable and most astrictive materials in the history of man are treasured up in India only!' (Mark Twain, 1835–1910, US writer)

'Cinema in India is like brushing your teeth in the morning. You can't escape it.' (Shah Rukh Khan, Indian actor and film producer)

Involving the audience
'Tell me and I forget. Show me and I remember. Involve me … and I understand.' This proverbial statement by the American statesman and inventor Benjamin Franklin (1706–1790) is true for every kind of presentation. If you want to be a good and convincing speaker you have to get the audience involved by paying attention to

- the atmosphere,
- your voice and your body language,
- the interaction between you and your audience,
- the structure and content of what you are presenting.

1 Match aspects 1–4 with the appropriate strategies (a–o).

1 atmosphere	
2 body language and voice	
3 interaction	
4 contents	

a)	Say thank you.
b)	Use rhetorical questions.
c)	Take the audience seriously.
d)	Establish eye contact with the audience.
e)	Be polite and friendly.
f)	Be enthusiastic.
g)	Don't cross your arms.
h)	Use humour/make jokes.
i)	Use sign-posting.
j)	Make an appeal what they could contribute.
k)	Think about their knowledge level.
l)	Tell them that you are excited too.
m)	Ask them for questions.
n)	Speak loudly and clearly.
o)	Face the audience.

2 Discuss the strategies listed in **1** in class and add more if possible. Which of these strategies have you actually used, which can you imagine using in a future presentation – and how?

3 The following text is the end of a presentation. Fill in the gaps with phrases from the box.

'Well, ________________, ________________ have come a long way in the last ________________. I really have to admit that being with you here, despite the fact that I was ________________ when I stepped up to the stage, ________________________. ________________ what I have said before, I must come to the following ________________. First, this issue will keep us busy for the next decades at least. But it is we ________________. Shouldn't we ______________________________? Of course, as individuals, we can't change the world in a few days or even months. But as somebody much more famous than me once said every big thing starts with ________________.

________________________, I hope it is that the necessity of fair-trade is not only a question of a good conscience on our side but it is a global matter. ________________________, the affluent European and American societies have to take over responsibilities for the developing and threshold countries.

Finally, I would like to ask you if there are ________________________. Don't hesitate even if I might not be able to answer all of them in detail but I will try and do my very best.

And in the end the only thing that is left for me is ________________________.'

any questions • a small step • conclusions • do something • finally • if you remember one thing from today hour • it was a pleasure • ladies and gentlemen • really excited/nervous • summing up • to say thank you for your attention • undoubtedly • we • who are to react

Being prepared
Even though you may agree in principle that it is a good idea to ask for questions at the end of a presentation, you might secretly be a bit afraid of these questions because you think you may not be able to answer them. But don't worry: the most important thing to do is to imagine possible questions by your partners and/or the audience even while preparing your presentation. Ask yourself: which points might the others come up with? Or: what would you want to know if you were in the audience? That way you won't be taken unawares.
There are different ways of reacting to questions from the audience. You can simply answer them – this is probably the best and easiest way, admit (perhaps humorously) that you don't know the answer, ask a question back, try to gain time, use the answer to steer the conversation into another direction.

4 Read the following responses to questions. Which of the above-mentioned strategies do they use?

- 'Excuse me, but what do you mean by saying ...?'
- 'Are you referring to ...?'
- 'This is a very interesting aspect concerning the issue I was talking about.'
- 'That is an absolutely valid question, but if you look at it from another angle ...'
- 'Actually I haven't got a clue ..., but perhaps *you* can tell me more about it.'

Try to find four more phrases or sentences you could use when answering questions.

5 Find a partner. Take turns in asking each other one of the following questions. Use the strategies above to react to them.

- 'Will the EU be the same kind of organization in 20 years time?'
- 'What would you prefer: modern comprehensive schools or traditional grammar schools?'
- 'In your opinion, what is the future of nuclear energy?'
- 'According to your studies and opinion, should alcohol be totally prohibited?'
- 'After what you have said, can you think of any effective strategies to fight doping in sports?'
- 'Do you think the process of globalization should and can be stopped?'

1 Steps towards a successful presentation

Before you can actually give a presentation, you have to prepare it. Below you will find a number of steps towards a successful presentation. Read them carefully, discuss them with a partner and add at least one tip for each step from your own personal experience.

Step 1: Analyse your topic

If possible, choose your topic according to your interests. But even a topic that seems boring at first may have some surprising aspects.
Think about different aspects and important elements of your topic. Look at the 'Operator': what exactly are you asked to do? How long will you have to talk, who will you talk to and what does your audience already know about the topic?

My tip: ______________________________

____

Step 2: Research your topic

Use different sources and take notes carefully. Write down your sources.

My tip: ______________________________

____

Step 3: Prepare your talk

Check important phrases and sentences.
Don't just write your talk down so that you can read it off, but prepare index cards.
Prepare visual aids (maps, illustrations, transparencies etc.).
Try to make your presentation sound interesting – if you are not interested in it yourself, your audience will never be.

My tip: ______________________________

____

Step 4: Practise your talk

Try out what you will actually say in your presentation. Time your talk, so you know whether it's too long or too short. Practise in front of a mirror or deliver your talk to friends or family.

My tip: ______________________________

____

Step 5: Deliver your presentation

Introduce yourself and your topic and explain the structure of your talk.
Watch your body language and look at your audience.
Mind your way of speaking: don't hurry, speak loud and clearly.
Use sign-posting: say what stage you are at in your presentation and what you are going to talk about next.

My tip: ______________________________

____

____

Sign-posting
It is important that the audience always knows where they are in the presentation. They need to know its structure (so it's important that your talk actually has one) and what is coming next. The audience can only know this if you tell them. You can put up 'verbal signs' along the route, i.e. words and phrases like first of all, finally, next …
And don't forget the 'KISS rule': 'Keep it short and simple.'

2 The three parts of a presentation

Like many other texts, most presentations consist of three major parts. In the middle column below, write down what their different functions are and what kind of message each of them communicates. Enter useful phrases in the right column; you can find a selection of such phrases underneath. (You may want to copy this table.)

Part	Function, message	Useful phrases
Introduction		
Main body		
Conclusion		

Useful phrases: Finally, let me remind you of some of the issues we have covered. • Welcome, ladies and gentlemen. • Today, I would like to talk about … • I would like to divide my presentation into the following parts … • A good example of this is … • As a next step, I would like to come to … • If there are any questions, now would be the time to ask them. • My name is Tom Miller and I'm here to … • To sum it up, … • If you have a quick look at the handout in front of you …

3 Practice

Deliver a presentation on one of the topics below. Time yourself. Start off with about a minute, then try to lengthen your talk by including all the functions and messages that you have come up with in the table above (*The three parts of a presentation*).

- A person I admire
- My favourite film/book/work of art
- Fashion
- Saving the environment
- My future

Find your own style
Good speakers or presenters can establish contact with the audience by
- adapting their way of speaking to the people they are dealing with,
- creating a good atmosphere,
- including jokes or other forms of humour,
- making their presentations very lively or even personal.

Doing this is not easy. Whether you succeed or not very much depends on your audience and the situational context. You should find a style you are comfortable with and not try to imitate a comedian or a professional scientist.

Speeches vs. presentations
Writing out or giving a speech can only be successful if you know about the features of a good speech beforehand: you should be able to analyse a speech before making one yourself.
Many of the tips for a good presentation also work for speeches. But a speech has to rely almost entirely on the power of words and the way they are delivered. Because of this (and contrary to presentations in general) it is helpful to write out the complete text of your speech first, then deliver it as freely as possible.

1 Brainstorm important features of a good speech and add to them while going through this worksheet:

____

____

____

____

____

____

____

2 Go through the following excerpt of a speech by Barack Obama, delivered after his victory in the 2008 presidential election. Analyse the underlined features according to their form and function:

If there is anyone out there <u>who still</u> doubts that America is a place where all things are possible; <u>who still</u> wonders if the dream of our founders is alive in our time, <u>who still</u> questions the power of democracy, <u>tonight is the answer</u>.
It's the answer told by lines that stretched around schools and churches in numbers this nation has never seen; by people who waited three hours and four hours, many for the first time in their lives, because they believed that this time must be different; that their voices could be the difference.
It's the answer spoken by <u>young and old, rich and poor, Democrat and Republican, black, white, Hispanic, Asian, Native American, gay, straight, disabled and not disabled</u> – Americans who sent a message to the world that we have never been just a collection of individuals or a collection of Red States and Blue States; we are, and we will always be, the United States of America.
It's the answer that led those who have been told for so long by so many to be cynical, and fearful, and doubtful of what we can achieve <u>to put their hands on the arc of history and bend it once more toward the hope of a better day</u>.
It's been a long time coming, but tonight, because of what we did on this day, in this election, at this defining moment, <u>change has come to America</u>. […]
America, <u>we</u> have come so far. <u>We</u> have seen so much. But there is so much more to do. So tonight, let us ask ourselves – if our children should live to see the next century (…) <u>what change will they see? What progress will we have made?</u>
This is our chance to answer that call. This is our moment.
<u>This is our time</u> – to put our people back to work and <u>open doors of opportunity</u> for our kids; to restore prosperity and promote the cause of peace; to reclaim the <u>American Dream</u> and reaffirm that fundamental truth – <u>that out of many, we are one</u>; that while we breathe, we hope, and where we are met with cynicism and doubt, and those who tell us that we can't, we will respond with that timeless creed that sums up the spirit of a people: <u>Yes, we can.</u>
Thank you, God bless you, and may God bless the United States of America.

3 As a member of the students' council at your school you have to deliver a speech to all students, motivating them to take part in this year's environmental project 'Make Our School Green!'. You have already written an outline (see centre column below). One of your friends has added some tips (left and right columns). Try to include these into your speech, taking into consideration everything you learned from page 1 of this worksheet.

Tips	Outline	Tips
	Ladies and Gentlemen,	Address your audience directly and personally; here: schoolmates!
Catch your listeners' attention with a surprising idea, a joke, an interesting situation.	I want to tell you something about this year's school project.	
Why not include a rhetorical question or a catchy slogan ('Pamper plants!', 'Watch your waste!') or a quotation?	The heads of school and the students' council came up with the idea to make the school greener.	Include the audience by using pronouns like 'our' or 'we'.
What about a repetition, a quotation, alliteration or a parallelism?	This includes • sorting the waste, • using recycled paper, • taking used paper to the paper collection, • reducing on packaging material, e.g. for breakfast and lunch boxes, • taking better care of the plants, • and other things.	Add some descriptive adjectives to create images in people's minds Sign-post your speech by telling them what is to come next.
You could ask the audience for questions or other contributions.	In each class you should discuss possible actions in your morning meetings and then hand in your proposals to the students' council.	Appeal to the audience to take action! If you are not convinced why should they be?
	Thank you for your attention!	

4 Now write out your speech completely and prepare to deliver it. If you do not like the topic and want to write a new speech from scratch, you can choose from the following topics and write an appealing, convincing and perhaps even funny speech that you can present to your classmates.

– In a world of contact lenses and laser operations, why wear glasses?

– In a world of right-handers, why be left-handed?

– In a world of online chat rooms and dating sites, why fall in love on the street?

– In a world of text messages, e-mails and social networks, why write letters?

Mediation
Mediating means passing on information from one language into another. For instance, you can mediate from German into English and vice versa. The original text may be written or spoken, and, depending on the situation, you may want to mediate orally or in writing.
Oral mediation can be very demanding, no matter whether you are telling somebody about something you have read or something you have heard. You have to think and act pretty fast, because you have to speak, understand, sum up, transfer and perhaps to listen at the same time.
In oral mediation, it is important to identify the communicative situation carefully, because it determines the style and way you speak. Who are you speaking to? What is your relationship with him or her? What are the purpose and the message of your mediation?
Remember:
- Don't translate, only give the gist.
- Paraphrase German words you don't know the English equivalent of.
- Use gestures and body language to get your message across.
- Watch the reactions of the person(s) you are mediating for and react to them.
- If there is a speaker, you can ask him or her to slow down.

Almabtrieb – what's that?

On the internet you have come across the following text:

Der traditionelle Almabtrieb in der bayerischen Alpenregion ANJA BERGLER
Zu einer der schönsten Traditionen gehört in den Bergregionen Bayerns der alljährlich stattfindende Almabtrieb. Geht der Almauftrieb im Frühjahr meist mit Viehtransportern und dergleichen recht unspektakulär vonstatten, wird der Almabtrieb im Allgäu, auch „Viehscheid" oder einfach nur „Schaid" genannt, jedes Jahr zur Zeit des Erntedankfestes fast schon zelebriert. Allein im Allgäu gibt es mehr als 650 Almen, die noch mit Tieren und für die Käserherstellung bewirtschaftet werden. Die genauen Termine für den Almabtrieb schwanken hierbei regional und sind auch von der entsprechenden Witterung abhängig. Doch spätestens am 30. September sollte die Almsaison beendet sein und die Almhütten der Senner oder Sennerinnen können entsprechend winterfest gemacht werden.
War die Saison der Senner auf den Almen sehr erfolgreich, ist auch dem Vieh nichts passiert und sind keine Krankheiten oder Todesfälle aufgetreten, dann werden die Tiere festlich für den Weg in das Tal geschmückt. Besonders der Kopfschmuck ist eine ganz besondere Augenweide. Dieser besteht aus Alpenblumen und Tannenzweigen, bunt verziert mit kleinen Spiegeln, Bändern oder Schleifen. Während im Allgäu nur die Leitkuh einen Kopfschmuck erhält, wird in den anderen Gebieten Bayerns jede Kuh beim Almabtrieb entsprechend geschmückt. Natürlich darf auch die Glocke beim sogenannten „Aufkranzen" nicht fehlen, die das Vieh um den Hals trägt. Die Größe der Glocken hängt von der jeweiligen Rangordnung des Tieres ab. Selbst kleine Kälbchen erhalten teilweise bei Bedarf ein Schmuckutensil.
Durch das Läuten der Glocken sollten der Sage nach böse Dämonen, die sich auf dem Abtriebsweg befanden, vertrieben werden. Im Tal angekommen, wird die Herde von Besuchern und den Landwirten feierlich in Empfang genommen und anschließend in die jeweiligen heimischen Ställe getrieben. Hier verbleiben sie dann bis zum nächsten Frühjahr, ehe es wieder auf die Alm hinauf geht.

Imagine you want to tell somebody who doesn't speak any German about this text:
- the 10-year old daughter of your English host-parents,
- your English pen-friend,
- an English professor of ethnology.

What aspects would be the same because they are essential to the text and of equal importance to anybody you might be mediating for? What would need to be different, depending on who you are talking to? Choose one of the three situations, take notes if necessary and then mediate the text orally.

Starting a conversation and keeping it up

Dos and don'ts in conversations
You all know the situation: you have just met somebody new, now you want to say something – but suddenly your brain feels quite empty. The question 'Do you come here often?' sounds clichéd and doesn't always work.
When meeting somebody new, it helps to

- be nice and polite, smile and introduce yourself,
- exploit the situation by explicitly referring to it ('This is an interesting location.' 'What do you like about music/films/ concerts like this?' 'Are you also a friend of Tom's?'),
- try to find common ground ('Oh, you like football too?' 'I didn't know that you are a member of this club too.'),
- give positive feedback ('You are so right.') and ask open questions rather than Yes/No-questions,
- show interest in your partner – everybody likes to talk about him or herself,
- be specific, avoid generalizations.

Do *not*

- simply agree, instead you should add an opinion of your own ('You are certainly right, but ...'),
- just say 'I love music', you should say what kind of music you like and why.

1 Find somebody who …

Go around in your class and start short conversations with your fellow students. Below are some ideas for things to talk about.
Don't forget to be nice and polite and to ask correct questions. Take notes.

Find somebody who …

- has a pet. Find out more about it.
- once broke a leg or an arm. How did it happen?
- hates a special colour. Why?
- reads in special places. Why?
- doesn't have a TV at home. Does that cause any problems?
- has met a famous person. Who, where and when?
- is left-handed or knows any left-handed people. Does it make life difficult?
- loves porridge for breakfast.
- hates ice cream.

Report about some of your interesting findings in class.

2 Appointments

Make appointments with three of your classmates at 1, 2 and 3 o'clock. Copy the appointment card below. First fill in your own part: try to think of something interesting or funny. Start meeting your partners when your teacher tells you so.

	Me	**1 o'clock**	**2 o'clock**	**3 o'clock**
Name				
I like				
I don't like / I hate				
I'm special because				
I like speaking English …				

Present to your class what you have found out about one of the people you have met.

3 Topics for conversation

There are a lot of topics you can talk about even if you don't know your conversation partner very well. Find a partner and look at the following list of topics. You might imagine that you are not in your classroom but at an event. Discuss which of the topics each of you would feel comfortable with talking about in English and start a conversation on one or two of them.

Touchy topics
One of the 'golden rules' for conversation is not to talk about politics or religion, because these topics might be controversial, especially when abroad.

- your hobbies and interests
- the event you are both at
- the weather
- the place
- recent news
- your families
- your jobs or other activities
- people you are both acquainted with
- a concert, a film, a book you have come across
- other people at the event

4 Double circle

Form a double circle. Your teacher will allocate the places and/or situations below to every person in one of the circles. At a signal from your teacher you will meet a person in the other circle and then start a conversation. After a minute you will move clockwise and meet another person in a different place. Before you start, look at the tip box on the previous page again ('Dos and don'ts in conversations').

in a stadium	on the plane	in a bar	at the cinema	in the street
in the sauna	in a shop	in a restaurant	at a concert	after an accident
at the sale	at an auction	at the gym	in the staircase	in a queue

5 Keeping up a conversation – open questions

Look at the following questions which only allow for a yes or no-answer. Change them into open questions. You can also add a second question or use a statement with a question tag. Find a partner and take turns in asking and answering the new questions.

- Do you like football?
- Have you been to one of these concerts before?
- Do you live around here?
- Do you prefer living in the city too?
- Wouldn't you agree that the music is too loud?
- Isn't it nice here?
- Do you often go to the theatre?
- Shouldn't we do more for young people's education?
- Can you imagine working for that company?
- Have you watched an interesting film recently?

Ending a conversation

1 With a partner, match the following sentences. Different combinations are possible. Practise them and present them to your class.

> If you want to end a conversation, you should
> - be polite and friendly,
> - tell the person you have been talking to that you are moving on,
> - say goodbye,
> - use the person's name if you know it.

Partner A		Partner B	
a)	Well, I think I ought to be going, Tom, if I'm going to catch my bus.	1	It was nice meeting you too, Susan. Thanks for coming to visit us.
b)	Please excuse me. I would like to say hello to an old friend.	2	No problem at all. I'll give you a call when I'm back in the office on Monday.
c)	Thanks a lot. Anyway, it was really nice to finally meet you in person.	3	Well, it was a pleasure talking to you. Enjoy the party.
d)	That was a very productive meeting. Thank you for your help.	4	Oh certainly. I have to make a move too and have a quick word with Thomas.
e)	I have enjoyed talking to you, Peter. I hope to see you again sometime.	5	What a pity, but you are right. Thank you for coming around and have a safe trip back.
f)	I think I'll have to leave. My flight tomorrow is very early.	6	Oh, you are right. It's nearly midnight. I'll see you to the door.

2 When ending a conversation you can use certain phrases that have different functions and meanings. Even if they are not meant entirely truthfully and honestly, it is polite to use them. Match the following functions with the given phrases. Keep in mind that some of them are more personal, some more formal. Mark the ones that you can't use in every situation and explain why.

Functions
1 Saying that you have to go
2 Saying thank you
3 Expressing pleasure
4 Mentioning future contact
5 Saying goodbye

Phrases	
a)	Bye and take care.
b)	Do get in touch when you are around.
c)	Give my regards to your parents/friends/colleagues.
d)	Have a safe trip back home.
e)	Have a good day.
f)	I am afraid I should be on my way.
g)	I hope we can meet again.
h)	I really appreciate your support.
i)	I think I ought to go now.
j)	I'm looking forward to meeting you again.
k)	Sorry, I really have to get going.
l)	Thank you so much.
m)	Would you give me a call when you are in Berlin again?
n)	You were a great help.
o)	See you soon.

3 Together with a partner, pick one of the following situations and end a conversation, using phrases and sentences from above.

After a business meeting	At the end of a birthday party	After a job interview
Having delivered something	At the end of an exchange trip	Having met your parents-in-law
After meeting an old friend	At an office party	In a bar

1 Look at the following phrases. Decide whether they are used to a) ask for information, b) give information or c) ask for clarification.

Hello, I'm here on holiday and …

Sorry, could you tell me please …

Do you think you could give a hand …

Have I understood that correctly …

Let me just explain that to you …

Oh, that's not very hard to find …

Is it correct that …

Would you mind showing me …

Excuse me, I am totally lost and …

Can I interrupt you for a second and …

Being polite …
When asking somebody for help or information, it's in your own interest to be polite because you are the one who needs something from the other person.
But of course you should be just as polite when it's the other way round and it's you giving the information!

2 Find a partner and take turns in asking for the following pieces of information. If you need more or different facts, simply make them up. The words in the box below may help you.

- the price of something you want to buy
- the departure time of your train
- the availability of a ticket for a film in the cinema
- the opening hours of a local museum
- the address of an administrative office
- a special offer
- exchanging a purchase you don't like anymore
- an appointment with a doctor

… when asking for information
Use friendly phrases like
- 'Excuse me …',
- 'Please, …',
- 'I'm sorry to interrupt, but …',
- 'could' and 'would you mind …' rather than 'can',
- questions rather than statements,
- question tags ('This is the XY museum, isn't it?'),
- 'Thank you for your help' or 'Thanks a lot.'

How much is/are … • I'm booked on the train from … to … • Are there any tickets for … • Excuse me, when is the … open? • Could you tell me where … • Is there anything on offer? • Can you offer any special discounts for … • Where can I change … • It doesn't fit. • I got it as a present and … • Could I see the doctor tomorrow / in the coming week because I had an accident / I caught a cold / I have a serious headache / attack of hay-fever / …

3 Choose an institution in your home town or area that you know a lot about, e.g. a museum, a club, a cinema or your school. Imagine that you are the representative of that institution. Find a partner. Tell him/her which institution you represent and start an informational conversation.

… when giving information
Say things like
- 'Sure!' or 'Of course, no problem!'
- 'Well, just wait a minute. Let me think about it.'

Even if you can't provide help you should say so in a polite and friendly way:
- 'I'm sorry, I'm afraid I can't help you.'

4 Write down as many polite phrases as you can for asking someone to slow down, to repeat something or for further explanation. Say which of these phrases are rather informal or formal (add a tick ✓).

	fml.	infml.

5 Answer the following queries. You give the information in one situation, you need time to think about it in the second situation and you haven't got a clue in the third one – you decide!

- You are close to your school. An English-speaking person asks for the shortest way to the nearest pharmacy.
- A group of English students is visiting your hometown/home area. They don't have any plans for the weekend and ask you for help.
- A visitor from the USA has tried to withdraw money from a cashpoint, but his/her card was kept by the machine. He/she doesn't know what to do.

6 Partner A: You don't speak any German. You have picked up a leaflet about the Church of Our Lady in Dresden and want to know what it says, so you ask Partner B for help. Act out your conversation together.

Herzlich willkommen in der Frauenkirche
Die Frauenkirche begrüßt all ihre Gäste, die sich an der Schönheit des Raumes erfreuen wollen und die Botschaft der Kirche in sich aufnehmen möchten. Seien Sie herzlich willkommen und treten Sie ein. Besichtigt werden kann die Kirche zu Zeiten der Offenen Kirche. Wer sich für eine geführte Besichtigung oder weiterführende Informationen interessiert, findet eine Vielzahl unterschiedlicher Möglichkeiten sowohl im Kirchraum als auch im Besucherzentrum. Nutzen Sie aber auch die Gelegenheit, die wunderschöne Aussicht von der Aussichtsplattform zu genießen oder sich in einer informativen Ausstellung über die Geschichte und den Wiederaufbau der Frauenkirche zu informieren.

Speaking on the phone can be more difficult than having a face-to-face conversation, especially if it's a formal call. This is because
- you normally don't see your partner and you don't have any non-verbal support (e.g. facial expression),
- there can be technical problems,
- you have to react spontaneously,
- you need to know certain telephone conventions and these can be different in a different language,
- there can be misunderstandings, especially when conveying names, facts, dates, addresses or appointments.

1 Parts of a telephone conversation

Put the following parts of a telephone call into a logical order by adding numbers and match them with partner A (= the caller) or B. Discuss your solution with a partner and come to an agreement.

In which order (1, 2, ..., 9)?	Who's talking – A or B?	Part of the call
		taking a message for someone
		introducing oneself
		putting someone through
		asking to speak to someone
		overcoming (connection/communication) problems
		leaving a message for someone
		confirming information
		finishing the conversation
		answering the phone

2 Important phrases for making phone calls

a) Identify the parts of a call (cf. task **1**) the following phrases belong to.

1 Could you ask her to call Stephen when she's back in?
2 One moment, please. I'll put you through.
3 Would you like to leave a message?
4 Thank you for calling.
5 May I speak to Mrs Smith?
6 I'll talk to you again soon. Bye for now.
7 This is 450789, Tom speaking.
8 Please hold the line for a moment.
9 Let me repeat the dates, just to make sure.
10 Could you slow down a little bit, please?
11 You said that your name was John, didn't you?
12 Hello, this is Hans Miller calling.
13 Could you take down my number? I'm not sure she's got it.
14 This is XY Company, Judy Brown speaking. How can I help you?
15 I make sure he'll get the message.
16 Good afternoon, my name is Susan Bauer, I'm calling from Germany.
17 Would the HR manager* Mr Miller be available?
18 The connection is really bad. Could you call me back, please?

b) Work with a partner. Partner A uses one of the phrases, Partner B reacts to it. Take turns.

* *HR manager = human resources manager* Personalleiter/in

3 A business call

Put this mixed-up business call into the right order by adding numbers (1–10) in the left column. Then practice the dialogue with a partner and present it to your class.

	Tom:	That would be really nice. Could she call me back as soon as she's in the office again?
	Tom:	I'm sorry, I didn't understand that. Could you speak more slowly, please?
	Marian:	No problem at all. Thank you for calling. Goodbye.
	Tom:	Good morning. My name is Tom Müller. I'm phoning from Dresden, Germany. Could I speak to Ms Jones, please?
	Marian:	Hello, Mr Müller, I just learned that Ms Jones is out of the office today. She will only be back by the late afternoon.
	Tom:	Oh, that's a good idea. It's 0049 351 123456. Thank you for your help.
	Marian:	Oh, of course, excuse me please. I just said that Ms Jones is not in at the moment. She is in a meeting. Can I give her a message?
	Marian:	Hold the line for a moment. I'll put you through.
	Marian:	Good morning. Blue Grass Music Company. Can I help you?
	Marian:	Let me just see whether I put everything down correctly. You said your name was Tom Müller from Dresden/Germany and you wanted Ms Jones to call you back. As I don't have it on my display, let me take down your number again, just in case.

4 Messages

Leave a message on

a) a good friend's answering machine making arrangements for a night out (cinema/pub/football/…);
b) the answering machine of a repair company because your car/dishwasher/TV/… has broken down and you need somebody to fix it.

Leaving a message on an answering machine
Whenever you phone somebody you should be prepared that there might not be anybody to answer the phone personally and that you may need to leave a message on a mailbox or an answering machine. In order that you don't have to hang up the phone just because you aren't prepared to say anything, you should always be able to provide the following information:

- who is calling, – the time of your phone call,
- your reason for calling,
- what you are asking for,
- your phone number.

And, as always: it's polite to say good-bye!

5 Telephone conversations

Put your chairs back to back so that you will only hear the other person's voice and practice the following telephone conversations. Keep in mind all the telephone phrases you have learned so far. Take turns in being the caller (A) or the recipient of the call (B).

✂- -

Partner A

1	You want to invite your friend to a party. It will take place next weekend and will include a nice meal and some dancing afterwards. You know that he/she is rather shy and hesitant to come to such a party. Phone him/her and convince him/her to come.
2	You need a Bed & Breakfast in Stratford-upon-Avon for yourself and your friend for the next summer holidays at a reasonable price. Before you make the booking you need to find out these things from the local tourist information: – Are there any vacancies for the summer? – How much is a room per day? – Are there any special discounts for students? – Can they provide tickets for the Royal Shakespeare Theatre? Phone the tourist information for answers.
3	You have to stay in your office over lunch because there is a lot of work to do, so you want to order pizza. You want it delivered fast because you are hungry. You are allergic to cheese. The pizza boy has to ring the office because you have to open the security door for him. Ask whether you can pay by credit card.
4	You work for the German furniture store 'Design for your life'. You have ordered chairs and tables from an American designer. The delivery has arrived but obviously something has gone wrong, because your company was sent shelves instead. You are trying to phone the sales department to complain and arrange for a solution to this problem.

✂- -

Partner B

1	Your friend is going to invite you to a party. You are not sure whether you want to go, as you can't dance very well and don't like mass events. Answer the phone.
2	You work in the Stratford Tourist Information Centre and answer the phone. You can give the following information: – not a lot of vacancies left; recommend fast decision – between 30 and 60 £ per day (the cheaper ones are not within walking distance of the theatres though) – 10 % off for students, – theatre holidays between mid-June and mid-July
3	You work at the call centre of a pizza service and take your customer's orders. You have to tell your customer that it might take some time (more than half an hour) for delivery. Don't forget to ask for name and address of your customer. Paying by credit card is okay.
4	You work as the receptionist of the American designer studio 'Young American Artists'. Connect the customer to the correct office (sales department/customer complaints). Unfortunately there is no one in at the moment. Apologize and take a message. Find out what the complaint is about.

Everyday discussions
There are many situations in everyday life when a casual conversation turns into a discussion. Maybe you want to convince someone of something, or you have different opinions on an important topic. For instance, you might have a discussion with your parents about how much pocket money you should get, or you might talk with your friends about your favourite films, or you might disagree with your friends about a particular question. In a discussion like this you have to be quick on your feet. You have to listen carefully, react quickly and fire back.

1 With a partner, pick one of the following pairs. Decide who takes which side and start discussing the issue. What is better:

- day or night?
- summer or winter?
- blue or green?
- Santa Claus or the Easter bunny?
- glasses or contact lenses?
- the UK or the USA?

Try to use as many of the phrases and words given below as possible. Whenever you use one, tick it off. Your discussion is finished when all the words and phrases are ticked, but it should go on for at least two minutes.
After you have finished, choose another topic and start again.

☐ Wait a minute …	☐ You are right, but …	☐ I don't think …	☐ Honestly …
☐ The problem is …	☐ Certainly …	☐ If you ask me …	☐ Actually …
☐ From my point of view …	☐ I see your point, but …	☐ But you can't be serious …	☐ I can't agree with that …
☐ You are right to some extent …	☐ Yes, but …	☐ Let me just say …	☐ After all …

2 Evaluate your discussion. What was easy, what went all right, what was difficult?

	easy	**all right**	**difficult**
Finding arguments	☐	☐	☐
Finding suitable phrases	☐	☐	☐
Understanding my partner	☐	☐	☐
Reacting to my partner	☐	☐	☐
Getting into the discussion	☐	☐	☐
Time management	☐	☐	☐

What would have helped you in your discussion? Write down two tips. Share all your tips in class.

First tip: ______________________________

Second tip: ______________________________

3 Find a new partner. Pick one of the pairs you and your partner have not already discussed (cf. task 1 above). Take five minutes to prepare some ideas, arguments and phrases, then discuss. If you are very brave you can even discuss in front of your class!

Taking sides or staying neutral
In any spontaneous or organized discussion, you may have one of the following roles:
You may be a *participant*, supporting a particular side in the discussion, either because you have been assigned this part (e.g. in a role play or a panel discussion) or because this is what you think anyway.
Or you are impartial, as the *chair* or *moderator*. You do not take sides. You start the discussion, keep it going and sum up the results. When things get heated, you have to remind the participants to stay calm and respectful.

1 You are going to chair a discussion on the following topic: 'Mobile phones: should they be banned in schools?'
Invent a real-life situation which might lead to such a discussion. Give roles to at least four of your classmates. Introduce them and their backgrounds, make them give introductory statements. Develop an introduction for the discussion.

2 The following things can happen in the discussion you are chairing. Write down possible reactions to get your participants back on track in a friendly and respectful way.

What's going on?	**I'm the chairperson – what should I do?**
The discussion dwells on one aspect for too long.	
The discussion seems to get repetitive.	
There are some participants who haven't said anything so far.	
One participant has been talking for too long.	
One participant is constantly interrupted.	
One participant is complaining that you do not give him/her the right to speak.	
Another participant is giving very evasive answers.	
One participant is accusing you of being biased.	

3 As a chairperson you should also sum up and close the discussion. Imagine you have discussed the topic mentioned in task **1**. Write out a short conclusion speech.

4 From what you have learned so far and from your own experience, write down three tips for a good chairperson.

First tip: ____________________

Second tip: ____________________

Third tip: ____________________

5 As a participant in a discussion, you should use your right to express your opinion so that the discussion can develop. Remembering all the speech acts and phases in conversation, write out possible contributions to the discussion on mobile phones (cf. task **1**). You can agree, contradict, express your opinion etc.

6 In groups of at least five, perform the discussion.

Speech acts in communication

Speech acts
Any communication consists of comparable parts or episodes. These are called *speech acts*. In a specific communication, the one or the other speech act may be more prominent (e.g. contradicting in an argument) and may thus be repeated, while others may not occur at all. Often, speech acts follow the same structure and use the same terms or sentence structures. You need to have an adequately wide register of words and sentences to be able to communicate fluently about different topics with different partners and in different situations. Collect useful phrases and sentences in an extra part of your folder or vocabulary book. Add to your list whenever you come across interesting terms.

1 Match the following speech acts with their explanations and put them in a logical order.

Speech act	What you do
1 Adding, backing up	a) You either introduce the situation or explain the topic.
2 Agreeing	b) You elaborate your arguments concerning the topic.
3 Asking for clarification	c) You invite your partner to speak if they haven't contributed a lot to the conversation so far.
4 Contradicting	d) You politely say that you have an opposing or a different opinion.
5 Expressing one's opinion	e) You try to find your way into the conversation without cutting your partner short.
6 Gaining time to think, fudging	f) You aren't sure that you've understood your partner correctly.
7 Interrupting	g) You need time to think or work on your argumentation.
8 Involving a partner	h) You bring the conversation to an end (e.g. by mentioning important aspects, establishing a compromise etc.).
9 Starting a conversation	i) You express that you are of the same opinion as your partner.
10 Summing up	j) You underline your partner's arguments and elaborate on his/her ideas.

2 Match the following phrases and sentences with the speech acts from **1** and explain your decision: Sorry to interrupt you, but … (_7_) – It seems to me that … (___) – Excuse me, I didn't quite catch that … (___) – Is there anything you would like to add? (___) – That's not the way I see it. (___) – So, to sum up … (___) – Well, now, let me see … (___) – Today's topic seems to be very controversial. Why don't we … first? (___) – You are absolutely right there (___) – I actually have to agree, and what makes it even more important … (___)

3 Together with a partner look at the phrases on the following page. If you don't understand what they mean, help each other or check with a dictionary. Match the phrases with the speech acts from **1**.

You can write these phrases or sentences on little strips of paper and use them as a 'discussion fan' to practise them in conversations. Don't forget to copy them into your list of discussion and conversation vocabulary.

Recently, I heard somebody … (_9_)	How do you feel about …? (___)	That's not the way I see it. (___)
I'm convinced that … (___)	How about you? (___)	To me … (___)
That is true to a certain extent, but … (___)	May I interrupt you for a moment, please … (___)	Do you mean ...? (___)
Sorry, could you say that again, please ... (___)	Well, I would say ... (___)	It's difficult to say exactly, but … (___)
If I understood the question correctly, … (___)	The general trend seems to be ... (___)	To cut a long story short … (___)
In brief … (___)	May I interrupt? (___)	What's more ... (___)
That illustrates perfectly what I would like to say ... (___)	This proves what X was saying/ you have been saying ... (___)	Here's a good example of what I mean ... (___)
I totally agree to what X has just said/you have just said ... (___)	Excuse me, I would like to add that ... (___)	I think ... is absolutely/you are absolutely right ... (___)
I take your point, but ... (___)	Did you really mean to say that ... (___)	I see what you mean, but I don't believe ... (___)
Can you give an example for that, please? (___)	If I understood you correctly ... (___)	Another thing is ... (___)
On top of that ... (___)	We must also consider ... (___)	I would like to add that ... (___)
That statement is true/right/ correct, because ... (___)	Some are in favour of ..., others against ..., but in general you can say that ... (___)	I don't know whether that is leading into the correct direction, but ... (___)
We have seen/heard that ... (___)	I don't go along with ... (___)	That may be true, but ... (___)
We also need to consider ... (___)	Sorry, but can I stop you for a moment? (___)	Unfortunately, I take the opposite view. (___)
With respect, I see the situation differently. (___)	That's all I wish to say about ... (___)	I'd like to bring this to a close with ... (___)
Having heard all these different views ... (___)	Well, I must admit you have a point here. (___)	It isn't as simple as that. (___)
I strongly believe that ... (___)	In my opinion ... (___)	It's a fact that ... (___)

If you ask me ... (___)	It cannot be denied that ... (___)	It's not as simple as that. (___)
Have you ever thought about ... (___)	I was really surprised to find out that ... (___)	You do have a point there. (___)
I think you are on the wrong track there. (___)	Oh sorry, I didn't catch that. (___)	I'm afraid I didn't follow. (___)
I couldn't have put it better myself. (___)	I hadn't thought of that. (___)	So, shall we agree to disagree? (___)
What a great idea! (___)	I don't think I would go along with this. (___)	To cut a long story short ... (___)
You are completely wrong assuming ... (___)	What is your view on the matter? (___)	

4 Using phrases from **2** or **3**, form at least ten sentences and try them out in a conversation with your partner.

5 Chain exercise

The proposition is: 'Red is the most horrible colour in the world.' Everybody in class has to agree or disagree and give a reason for his/her opinion without repeating any of the phrases or reasons given before.

6 Spotlight

Form groups of five or six. In each group, find a volunteer who dares to sit in the spotlight. The volunteer must pretend to hold an unpopular opinion on a certain issue. He or she could be a supporter of a particular football club, a fan of a very special kind of music or dislike something that is very popular among most people. Start a discussion with him/her, convincing him/her of your opinion. Stay polite, but support each other in your argumentation.

7 Three-minute discussion

Together with a partner prepare a three-minute discussion on one of the following keywords: love – mobile phones – family values – friendship – childhood. For the sake of discussion take opposing views and contradict each other. Try to find a good introduction, use phrases listed above (**2** and **3**) and try to come to suitable conclusion.

Role plays in foreign language learning
Using role plays or simulations to activate the learner is a method that you might have come across in many subjects, e.g. in social studies or history and politics. In foreign languages, however, the main focus is on language and interaction strategies. You use these to create your part and join in the discussion about an issue.
The skills to be successful in role-plays are
- mainly speaking skills like in 'normal' conversations, discussions and debates;
- being able to interpret a role (card) fast and spontaneously;
- some presentation or dramatic skills to play a part that is different from your own character and opinion.

Role plays can take the form of a normal dialogue, but you may also be asked to simulate a panel or radio discussion.

1 Role play (introductions)

Read the following mini-role cards, pick one quickly and introduce yourself. Invent some further details about your person (interests, hobbies, opinions ...) that might fit.

Mary Miller, 46, American high school teacher, married, two children	James Barker, 21, student at the London School of Economics, football supporter
Jim Clarke, 65, retired farmer from Wales, proud grandfather of seven grandchildren, amateur singer in a choir	Susi Sorrow, 17, left school after GCSEs, dreams of becoming famous
Tim Taylor, 18, high school student from Iowa, captain of the school football team	Petula Porter, 54, housewife from Wisconsin, active member of different social clubs in her hometown
Bill Doors, 38, San Francisco, computer specialist and owner of the San Francisco 49er Football Club	Peter Müller, 16, German exchange student in Illinois, originally from Frankfurt/Main

2 Invent a role card for yourself where you write down your (new) name, your hometown, your age, a job, a hobby and your favourite colour.
Stand up, walk about the room and start conversations with as many people as you can, trying to find out interesting facts about your partners. Present some interesting findings to your group.

3 Form a double circle. If you haven't met the person opposite you before quickly exchange the most important facts. Imagine you have some sort of relationship: what is it, how, where and when did it start? Present your stories to the group.

4 Balloon game

Form groups of six. Draw lots (or throw the dice) to decide who you are. You are all together in a hot-air balloon which is about to crash. Not all of you can stay on board, because the basket is too heavy. Convince the others why you have to stay.

Adele (born 1988), award-winning British singer-songwriter	Albert Einstein (1879–1955), German-American physicist, developed the theory of relativity
Charles Lindbergh (1902–1974), American aviator and author, crossed the Atlantic Ocean in his plane in a solo non-stop flight in 1927	Marilyn Monroe (1926–1962), American actress, singer and showgirl, starring in successful films like *Some Like It Hot* (1959)
Sigmund Freud (1856–1939), Austrian neurologist who founded the discipline of psychoanalysis	Bill Gates (born 1955), founder of the computer company Microsoft, author and billionaire

5 Role play (dialogue)

Find a partner. Pick one of the following situations and decide which part you want to play in it. Present your dialogue to the class. You should discuss for at least three minutes.

Situation 1
You are boyfriend and girlfriend. After some months of a happy relationship the boy suddenly called the girl and asked for a meeting. Now he is dumping her all of a sudden.

Situation 2
You are at home either relaxing or doing something that is really important when a sales rep appears at your doorstep and wants to convince you to buy a product.

6 Role play (discussion): A year abroad in Germany

Form groups of six. Pick one of the role cards and make yourself familiar with your part. Add ideas if they help you to present your person more convincingly in the discussion. In the discussion, try to arrive at a solution or compromise which everybody can agree on. You should discuss for at least for six minutes.

Role 1
Joshua/Jody Miller, 16, from St. Paul, Minnesota, high school student, wants to spend a year in Germany to learn the language and get to know the country of his/her grandparents

Role 2
Mary Miller, 44, J's mother, basically approves of his/her plans, but: anxious, afraid of intercultural problems, first time her son/daughter would be away for such a long time

Role 3
Frank Miller, 48, J's father, absolutely enthusiastic about the chance that is offered to his son/daughter, problems with financial support, afraid that it might affect marks in the USA badly when coming

Role 4
Tom Masterson, 56, high school principal, very balanced view on advantages and disadvantages of such an enterprise; doesn't want to lose J., because he/she is head girl/boy of the school and team

Role 5
Vicky Tucker, 32, representative of the exchange organization, can provide necessary information on prices, grants, risks and experience

Role 6
Susan Evans, 36, school guidance counselor. J. asked her to mediate the discussion, because it has become rather heated

Debating – rules and roles
A debate is a formal confrontational discussion following fixed rules. Every debate has a *chair*. He or she is neutral, welcomes the audience, introduces the teams and the motion, announces the vote and closes the debate.
You start off with a *motion* which is the controversial topic of the debate. It is always formulated as *'This house believes …' (THB)*. The debaters are then divided up into two sides, *proposition* and *opposition*, each having to find valid arguments for their side even if they personally don't agree with it. Usually there are two to four speakers for each side, who are taking turns in proposing or opposing the motion in a previously fixed time which is checked by the so-called *time-keeper*. After a short break in which the discussion can be opened to the *floor* (i.e. the audience) this argumentation is followed by *rebuttal or reply speeches* of each side which may be slightly shorter than the speeches before.
After the debate either the house (i.e. everybody present) or a *panel of judges* votes to decide who won the debate. They take into account who provided the better arguments and who spoke more convincingly. Again it is not important what their/your personal opinion is.
During the speeches the other team can introduce *points of information (POIs)*, i.e. ask questions or comment on something. These can be turned down, but if they are accepted, they must be answered immediately.

1 Form groups of four. Agree on a set of motions you would like to debate. They can be serious ('THB that voting age should be lowered.') or funny ('THB that Santa Claus should wear green clothes.'). Keep in mind that they have to be controversial and you should find them interesting.

____

____

____

Decide and explain to your group why you would rather be on the proposing (i.e. supporting the motion) or opposing side.

2 Fill the gaps in the following introduction and conclusion of the chair. Deliver it to your class:

'Ladies and Gentleman, welcome to this debate. The motion for today's debate is ____________________. The teams debating are ____________________ which is proposing and ____________________ which is opposing. Speaking for the proposition are ____________________, ____________________ and ____________________. Speaking for the opposition are ____________________, ____________________ and ____________________. The reply/rebuttal speeches will be done by ____________________ and ____________________. Please welcome them. Our timekeeper today is ____________________. Speaking time for the speeches today is ____________________. The judges for this debate are: ____________________, …

I declare the proposing/opposing side the winner of today's debate [mention the motion again] and declare the debate closed.'

3 Find a partner to read out the following argument to you. Listen carefully and try to introduce two POIs at reasonable points by standing up and saying 'Point of information' and developing his/her ideas. Your partner should try and answer them. Swap roles afterwards and try again. Remember to stay polite and fair. A debate is always about respect for other opinions.

> Ladies and gentlemen,
>
> The proposing side believes that Germany needs a monarch and our case today rests on three main points:
>
> First, many countries in the world are still successfully ruled by a monarch. Second, the current political situation in Germany calls for a monarch. And third, a monarch would be a suitable role model for identification.
>
> In the first place we would like to draw your attention to the fact that there are several democratic countries in Europe and the world that are ruled by constitutional monarchy at the moment. One only has to consider the United Kingdom, Sweden or Denmark in Europe to see that democratic values and a solid constitution can be supported and developed under the rule of constitutional monarchy. You only need to ask the people in these countries to find out that, despite all conflicts and modern developments, monarchy guarantees the uniting power of history and tradition.
>
> Second, nobody needs to be reminded how tired of politics and politicians Germans have become in recent times. There seems to be an on-going process of not telling the truth, being involved in dubious affairs and so on. The traditional figurehead of a monarch would bring relief and an end to this negative development.
>
> And last but not least, having a monarch would bring back a symbolic role model and a long-lost centre of identification to the German population.

4 Develop one good argument in favour and one against each of the following motions.

This house believes that …
- the Olympic Games should be abolished.
- single-sex education should be promoted.
- the world should speak one language.
- computers cause more harm than good.
- sports are harmful to your body and soul.

First with a partner and then with another pair, exchange and evaluate your arguments in order to find out which ones are most convincing. (You may want to use the Think-Pair-Share method to do this.)

5 Make sure that you understand the rules of a formal debate. Divide the roles among your group. You need a chair, a time-keeper, about three speakers each for proposition and opposition and a panel of judges. The rest of the class are the floor. Decide whether they should be allowed to ask questions and/or vote.

Choose one of the motions you have developed above (cf. **1** and **4**). Take about ten minutes for preparation, then start your debate.

Don't forget to vote for the winner in the end.

Roles in an interview
Even if you aren't a famous person and never will be, you might still be interviewed, e.g. when applying for a job. In an exam or in a mock interview, you may also be asked to take over the part of the interviewer.
When you are interviewed, the following tips might be helpful:
- Prepare for the interview and try to imagine what you might be asked.
- Try to relax and take your time, but don't fall silent.
- Answer in full sentences. Take initiative rather than staying passive.
- Listen to the questions carefully, because you can use parts of them in your answers.
- Ask back, if you don't understand the question.

If you are the interviewer
- prepare for the interview by finding something out about the person you are going to interview.
- Create a pleasant atmosphere by starting with an easy question.
- Ask W-questions, i.e. open questions that give the person interviewed the opportunity to develop their answer.

If both partners in an interview interact well, a formal interview may turn into a fruitful conversation.

1 a) Write down interview questions to which the following might be the answers:

Yes, I did.
This is absolutely correct.
No, not at all. It is playing football.
I can live with both, but I prefer the first.
I actually don't want to answer that question.
Giraffes and hippos.
I don't care much about that issue.
A set of books, music and a hamburger.
Never in my life.
That was the weirdest thing that has ever happened in my life and it changed it totally.

b) Practise the interview with your partner and present it. You can make answers longer and insert more questions, if you want to.
c) Based on this interview, write a short description of the person interviewed.

2 Write down five questions you would like to be asked in an interview. Find a partner, exchange your questions and interview each other. Tell your class something interesting you found out about your partner.

3 **Hot seat**

You are going to be interviewed by your classmates.

a) As they probably know a lot about you already, tell them about a special detail (e.g. a weird hobby or interest, a rare skill, an unusual holiday) or invent something special that you have done, experienced, come across or bought recently and invite them to ask questions on that issue.
b) You are not allowed to answer truthfully. Try to stay consistent nevertheless.

4 Together with a partner, research the biography of a famous or important person on the internet. Make up a fictitious interview and present it to the class.

5 Very little is known about William Shakespeare. In a group of three or four, collect what you know about him, then think of interview questions and fictitious answers. Present your interview with Shakespeare to the class.

6 Look at the following questions which you might hear in a job interview. Together with a partner speculate what they could be aiming at. Then take turns in answering them.

- What do you believe to bring to this job?
- What did you like best/least about your last job?
- Are you more of a creative thinker or a structured planner?
- Where do you see yourself five years from now?
- Apart from your qualifications, what personal assets can your offer us?
- Why should I hire you?
- What is your favourite working environment?
- What motivates you to show your greatest effort?
- What do you know about our company?
- Do your prefer working alone or in a team?
- What is your most successful experience in your work life?
- How would you react to a serious mistake you have noticed somebody else making on the job?

Make up more questions you might be confronted with.

Job interviews
In a job interview the interviewer is not only interested in your personality but foremost in your qualifications, your motivation for the job, your professional strengths and weaknesses, ability for cooperation and teamwork and your plans for the future. When applying for a job, a grant, a scholar-ship or a place at university it is important to be prepared and to try to maintain a conversational flow.
You should
- be informed about the company or institution you are applying for. Put yourself 'on the team' by mentioning the company's or the interviewer's name,
- be able to give further information about facts and qualifications you mentioned in your CV and application,
- include concrete data; you should not talk generalities,
- repeat your strengths and include little success stories without boasting,
- pay attention to your behaviour and body language,
- follow a given dress code,
- watch your language and be outspoken, but always polite and friendly.

7 You are looking for an internship. On the internet, you have found the following job offer:

Design for Fashion Label, New York City
For more than 30 years, our company has been designing knitwear with flair. Located in the heart of the garment district, our label now boasts a contemporary line, Smitten. The inspiration for Smitten was born from our designers love for retro romance comic books from the 1940s and 50s. Their design studio is adorned by these classic American romance images, which inspire them season after season.

Learning experience to include the following responsibilities:
- assist sales team with developing & maintaining buyer relationships,
- track samples (check in/out samples, organize shipments, etc),
- maintain showroom appearance,
- organize press materials (press kits, look book mailings, etc),
- participate in various trade show events; help with sales, organize/steam garments, etc,
- update database with vendor information,
- filing, data entry and general fashion showroom responsibilities.

This position is within our corporate office which also houses our design team and New York showroom. This is unique as it affords the opportunity to experience fashion from the inception of design to the fruition of a full, saleable collection. We are looking for someone honest, intelligent, who enjoys fashion, and wants to learn about the industry.
Hours: Minimum 20 hours per week, days and hours flexible upon intern's schedule.
While flexible, interested applicants should be prepared to treat this position as a job. STIPEND: 20$ clothing allowance per 8 hours work (cumulative time), 20$ CASH per 8 hours work.

Split the class in halves and prepare for the job interview, using the role cards you will be given. All members of your group should practise the interview with their partners. Some groups should present it in front of class. All the others listen and assess the interviews. Who was the best interviewer and who would you give the job to? Explain your decision.

✂- -

Role card 1

You are the interviewer: Hugo di Fabrio, Human Resources Manager (*Personalleiter*).

You are 35 years old and have worked in the fashion industry for quite some time. You are interested in creative, open-minded young people with an international approach.

→ Take notes on questions you would like to ask the applicant. Here are some ideas:

- What kind of candidate are you looking for?
- Which qualification must he/she offer?
- What about her/his language abilities?
- What are her/his experiences/ideas in fashion and design?

✂- -

Role card 2

You are the applicant for the internship.

You want to start working after having your school-leaving exam. You have some previous experience because fashion and design is one of your favourite hobbies and you have already done some internships in school holidays. You also want to broaden your cultural horizon and would love to spend time in New York.

→ Think of qualifications and skills you could offer that are useful for the job. Make up some questions you would like to ask the human resource manager. Why should he hire exactly you for this internship?

✂- -

Politeness in conversations

Being polite
If you want to be polite in English-speaking conversations you should follow certain rules, some of which may seem unusual to non-natives:

- Never simply say 'yes' or 'no' or answer with just one word. Instead, use short answers or concessional phrases like 'I actually don't think so', 'I know what you mean, but ...', 'You are right to a certain extent; however, from my point of view, ...'
- Don't talk in monologues, but try to involve your conversation partner, e.g. by using question tags, asking questions about his family or hobbies etc.
- Use downtoners to avoid German bluntness: 'it's just', 'not really', 'not totally', 'a little bit', 'maybe':
- Intersperse your conversation with feedback phrases and terms of politeness like 'I'm sorry', 'Thank you very much', 'I really appreciate that', 'Oh, really', 'That is surprising', 'Oh well', 'I see what you mean' etc.
- If you want to express enthusiasm, use emphatic devices like 'I really do believe ...', 'I'm totally convinced ...' or 'What an extraordinarily nice dinner!'

Of course, often it is not only about the words or phrases you use. The tone, pronunciation and body language you give to them are also important.

1 Do you consider the following phrases as impolite (–), neutral (O) or polite (+)? Discuss with a partner and explain your decision.

Accept that? No way!	
Some more precise ideas would be really helpful.	
Oh no! You can't be serious.	
I'd like to think it over again, if that is okay with you.	
Just give me the box! I need it.	
I strongly object.	
You are wrong.	
I'm so hungry I can't take it anymore.	
I don't care.	
Would you mind if we took a short break?	
I actually wouldn't mind any of your alternatives.	
I'm sorry, but I don't think that's quite correct.	

2 React politely to the following friendly remarks. (Remember: the other person doesn't want to be told the story of your life.)

Hi – how are you?
Do you come here often?
Isn't it a wonderful day today?
Any plans for the coming weekend?
Are you enjoying yourself here?

3 **Hot seat – don't say 'yes' or 'no'**

Form groups of four or five. Take turns in being asked questions about things you like or dislike, hobbies, family etc. Don't answer with 'yes' or 'no', but use every other possible form of replying. Time each other. The one who 'survives' longest has won.

4 Asking back, reacting to something

Look at the following situations. How could you say yes and how could you reject the request? Write down a polite response as well as a very direct or even rude answer. Compare your answers and try them out with a partner, also using different kinds of intonation and body language.

- A not very close friend, who is always borrowing money from others, asks you for some money.
- You are in a hurry. Your next door neighbour who is 85 years old desperately asks you to give her and her luggage a lift to the station because the taxi hasn't shown up and her train will leave soon.
- Your boss asks you for your opinion on a new project. You are not very convinced of it.

5 Florian is a German student staying with an American family. His hosts are asking him some questions and are making some suggestions. Read Florian's answers and make them sound more polite.

Hosts: Would you like to go to a concert with us?
Florian: No, I don't like music.

Hosts: What about going swimming at the weekend?
Florian: No, I think it's too cold.

Hosts: Would you like to join us for a trip to the mountains?
Florian: Yes, can you pick me up in town?

Hosts: I'm just going shopping. Can I get anything for you?
Florian: No, but you can take me with you. I will buy my stuff myself.

Hosts: What would you prefer for dinner, spaghetti or roast beef?
Florian: I don't care.

Hosts: Would you like some more potatoes and sauce?
Florian: No, I'm full.

Intercultural communication

Whenever communicating with someone with a different cultural background, you should briefly analyse the situation:

- What message do you want to convey: do you want to inform, accept or turn something down? Are you trying to convince somebody, do you have to defend yourself, etc.?
- What is the relation between you and your conversational partner? Are you on the same level, or does one of you have more authority or power and thus deserves more respect?

Adapt your style and register to the situation:

- Use either more formal or informal terms and sentences, as appropriate.
- Adapt your register: are you talking to a child, a young person of your peer group, your boss, somebody from a high-tech company, ...?

Avoid stereotypes. They are not helpful for an enjoyable conversation.

6 Find a partner and act out one of the following conversational situations in a polite and culturally acceptable way. It may be helpful to take some notes before and look at the tips again.

a) You are at an American High School for an exchange year. You know that being at school on time is an extremely important rule at this school. You arrive late in the morning and are being told off by the principal who sees you coming in. You could blame it on your host brother who slept in this morning, but you don't want to let him down, because he is at the same school.

b) You are doing an internship at a British company. Your boss invites you for lunch and starts talking about British and German attitudes towards the EU. As far as you know, the British feel rather sceptical about EU, but you don't know much about this and you don't want to sound rude.

c) You get on an ICE train to Munich and find your reserved seat taken by an English-speaking family with some children. The train is absolutely packed. Talk to them to find a solution.

Spoken language – everyday English

Spoken vs. written English
The level and style of language ('register') that we use varies with the situation and people involved. Of course you can use many of the words, phrases and sentences that you use in your written English in spoken English too. Nevertheless, there are some special features of spoken English that you can use in your presentations, in discussions and conversations as long as you don't overdo it.
Spoken English is generally more informal than written English. It uses

- shorter sentences (mostly main clauses),
- short forms,
- fillers (well, to my mind, I suppose, you know etc.)
- repetitions,
- vague expressions (kind of …, something like that, like, sort of),
- a more emotional tone which can be expressed by language emphasizers (question tags, adverbs, exclamations, inversion), body language and intonation.

Not every spoken context is alike, though. There is a difference between chatting with a friend and having a business discussion with your boss, so that sometimes you can use a more informal kind of everyday English and at other times you have to be more formal.

1 Especially when agreeing and disagreeing you can either use direct and informal phrases or stay on a more formal level. Look at the following phrases and enter them into the grid below.

I entirely agree. • Nonsense! • I'm so stupid. I was totally wrong. • I'm totally with you there. • You must be joking. • I have to apologize, I didn't take that into account • You hit the nail on the head. • Well, not a bad idea. • I wonder if we shouldn't … • I can't believe you said that. • I have to contradict you here. • Fine with me. • That doesn't seem convincing to me. • Sorry, I can sometimes be such an idiot. • No way. • You what? • I find that hard to believe. • I suppose some people might see it like that.

	formal	informal
Agreeing		
Disagreeing		
Admitting that you are wrong		

2 Make the following statements sound more convincing by adding 'emphasizers'. Example:

It makes a difference. → It does make a (big/tremendous/enormous) difference. / It makes a difference, doesn't it? / It actually makes a difference. / I beg your pardon, it makes a difference.

Practice saying them with and without your additions.

> You are right. • I agree. • I have never experienced that. • It takes many years to do that. • I believe that. • You are confronted with the same problems. • You are wrong. • This is alarming. • I find that surprising. • That could be true.

3 Change the following very formal speech into a more informal one that you would direct at people you are more closely acquainted with in a more relaxed situation. Look at the tip box again to find out which aspects you could work on. Present your speech to your class.

> Ladies and Gentlemen,
>
> It is my pleasant duty to welcome you all to this wonderful and memorable event of the 25th anniversary of our foundation. Allow me to start the evening by introducing the most honourable and laudable president of our partner club, Mr. Saddler. A long-pending desire has been fulfilled today with his presence, even more so as he is also accompanied by his wonderful wife, Mrs. Saddler. Let us all welcome them in our midst with a warm applause.
>
> If in the course of the evening you would like to indulge in the delicious luxuries offered by the kitchen of this house you are cordially requested to move to the adjoining room. Should any of the planned parts of tonight's programme fail to meet your full satisfaction, which appears to be highly improbable, let me know immediately. We will try our very best to meet and even exceed your expectations.
>
> I hope you will all have a pleasant evening.

Spoken vs. written English
Speaking – not one, but several skills
Speaking is different from other foreign-language learning skills. Not everything in your spoken English can be judged according to the categories of right or wrong, nor can mistakes always be tracked down and marked individually as in, for instance, written assignments.
What always counts, of course, is contents. This is especially true for presentations, where you are the only one who is speaking. You have to talk about the topic and cannot digress from it.
But there are other important aspects of speaking which are perhaps even more important: your language skills, your forms of interaction, the communicative structure you lend to your presentation or interaction.
You should be aware of these different aspects of speaking, because each may be evaluated in class as well as in exams.

1 Look at the following table and assess your speaking skills (add a tick ✓). Try to be honest with yourself. If you are not sure ask one of your classmates or the teacher for his/her assessment.

	Yes	Well, sort of ...	No
People understand me when I talk in a presentation, to a partner or in a group.			
I can understand others and react to what they say.			
I speak fluently. When I don't know a word I can paraphrase it.			
I have a sufficient range of communicative vocabulary to interact with other people.			
I can react spontaneously to different kinds of cues.			
I can carry on a conversation and follow a line of argument.			
I can be convincing without being unfriendly or appearing aggressive.			
If there is a break, gap or problem in the conversation, I know how to react.			
I can use adequate body language and gestures.			
I have a suitable time management.			
I can deal with (my) nervousness and feel confident enough to speak in front of other people.			

2 When marking their students' speaking skills, teachers often use evaluation tables. Look at the one below which describes excellent performance in all aspects of speaking.

contents	interaction/ teamwork	language correctness	style
total perception of the given situation topic aspects detailed, at adequate length and presented expressive-ly and convincingly	very flexible and skilful cooperation, balanced involvement of both use of paraphrases and changing of wording if necessary excellent guiding of the conversation	adequate speed, near-nativeness in pronunciation and intonation only few little mistakes which don't impair clarity or comprehensibility	complex sentence structures are often used and nearly always correct varied and complex vocabulary and idiomatic structures

On the basis of the evaluation table, formulate tips.

Use ______________________________.

Integrate ______________________________.

Prepare and practice ______________________________.

Don't ______________________________.

... ______________________________

3 Now think of a monologue situation, e.g. a presentation. How would the evaluation sheet have to be adapted? Which aspects can be dropped, which have to be added?

Speaking in test situations
Speaking is one of the most practical skills you acquire in your English lessons. It's a skill you need when asking for information, talking to somebody who doesn't speak German, communicating across cultures or even having a real job interview in English.
Some testing situations, whether in a school exam or when applying for a job, may appear rather artificial. There is always a certain degree of role-play expected of you, and this may make you feel uncomfortable at first.
Whether in an exam or in a real-life interview, you should be familiar with a few rules and observe certain structures that will help you not to be caught unawares:

- Collect and memorize useful vocabulary and sort it according to the different aspects and parts of the oral exam (e.g. phrases for presentation or phrases for discussion).
- Find out as much as you can about the test situation.
- Try to adapt to the situation as quickly as possible by using adequate style, register and suitable behaviour.
- If there is a prompt or a written task of some sort, analyse it carefully.
- Don't stop mid-sentence, but don't rush things either.
- If you need time to think, don't stay quiet, but say things like 'That is an interesting question', 'I've never thought about it that way', 'Let me think about that for a second ...' or 'Did I understand you correctly ...'.

The more you practise these things, the more comfortable you will feel.

1 Analyse the test situation

Look at the following overview of different test situations. What does each of them ask you to do?

Monologue

Independent: presentation on a particular topic (prepared or spontaneous)	Guided: presentation answering questions or reacting to a text

Dialogue

Communication with a teacher or exam panel in an interview, a discussion or a role play	Communication with partners (classmates, applicants)

Match the following tips with aspects of the testing situations above. Together with a partner, discuss the usefulness of these tips and add one or two more from your personal experience.

1. Prepare your material so that you can use it effectively (write down keywords only, use abbreviations, clear handwriting).
2. Negotiate with your partner (if possible beforehand) who is going to start, who takes the leading part, who forms a conclusion etc.
3. Practise with as many of your potential partners as possible.
4. Research for old exams and find out about the structure and possible tasks.
5. Practise questioning strategies.
6. Use presentation strategies by practising how to describe and analyse the most different elements and phenomena.
7. Visualize and describe various roles and parts in discussions (introduction, presenter, moderator, pro/con etc.).
8. If there is a set time frame, practise speaking for exactly that amount of time.

2 Analyse your task

Like most other exam tasks, speaking questions also use *Operatoren* that tell you what exactly you are supposed to do – provided you know what is meant by them. Look at the following list of *Operatoren* and match them with their explanations.

1 Assess/Evaluate	a) Weigh up both sides of an issue, come to a justified conclusion.
2 Comment on	b) Show certain (important) points of an issue clearly.
3 Discuss	c) Explain why something is as it is by giving significant aspects or examples.
4 Illustrate	d) Form an opinion by carefully weighing the pros and cons.
5 Interview	e) Analyse an issue and state your personal opinion on it.
6 Justify	f) Give the main features of a topic.
7 Outline	g) Obtain valuable and interesting information from the person asked.
8 Point out	h) Enumerate and explain adequate reasons for coming to a conclusion.

From the speaking and testing situations you have come across so far, find an example for each of the *Operatoren*.

3 Think positive

Some of you may say that they prefer written exams to oral ones. But actually, speaking tests have a lot of advantages:

- In a communicative exam you are not alone. There is always somebody who can help you.
- Unlike in a written exam, spelling doesn't matter.
- Speaking is something that you will really need in your future life.
- It is always more pleasant to talk to a real person than to communicate with a piece of paper.
- After all these *Klausuren*, here's your second chance.

With a partner, try and find some more positive aspects of spoken exams.

KV 2 Making contact with the audience

1 1 a, e, f, h, l; 2 g, n, o; 3 c, d, j, m; 4 b, i, k

2 ladies and gentlemen – we – hour – really nervous – it was a pleasure – summing up – conclusions – who are to react – do something – a small step – finally – undoubtedly – any questions – to say thank you for your attention

KV 3 Giving a presentation

2 Possible answers:

Part	Function, message	Useful phrases
Introduction	stating the topic catching the audience's attention establishing an atmosphere explaining complicated concepts or terms outlining the structure ...	Welcome, ladies and gentlemen. Today, I would like to talk about ... I would like to divide my presentation ... My name is Tom Miller and I'm here to ... ...
Main body	developing arguments or varied aspects of the topic connecting aspects stating pros and cons giving examples ...	A good example of this is ... As a next step I would like to come to ... If you have a quick look at the handout in front of you ... ...
Conclusion	summing up all aspects giving an outlook asking for questions ...	Finally, let me remind you ... If there are any questions, now would be ... To sum it up, ...

KV 4 Delivering a speech

2

	Form	Function
who still (3x)	repetition, parallelism	hammering in the message
tonight is the answer	climax, metaphor	conviction conveying an image and contributing to the atmosphere
young and old (...) disabled	enumeration	panoramic view including everybody
to put their hands ...	metaphors	emotional appeal, vivid image
change has come to America	personification	lending power to the idea
we	inclusion of audience	appeal, feeling as one
what change ...?	rhetorical questions	appeal; asking for involvement
This is our time	inclusion (also repetition)	unifying effect
open doors of opportunity	metaphor	vivid image
American Dream	concept	linking speech to history
that out of many, we are one	quotation ('e pluribus unum'), inversion	referring to American concepts of history and philosophy
Yes, we can.	slogan	reminding of common task

KV 7 Ending a conversation

1 Possible combinations: a 6, b 4, c 1, d 2, e 3, f 5
2 1 f, i, k; 2 l; 3 h, n; 4 b, c, g, j, m; 5 a, d, e, o

KV 9 Speaking on the telephone

1 Order / Who's talking?: 7/B – 2/A – 4/B – 3/A – 5/A or B – 6/A – 8/B – 9/A or B – 1/B;
2 a) answering the phone: 14; introducing oneself: 7, 12, 16; asking to speak to someone: 5, 17; putting someone through: 2, 8; overcoming problems: 10, 18; leaving a message for someone: 1, 13; taking a message for someone: 3, 15; confirming information: 9, 11; finishing the conversation: 4, 6
3 7 – 5 – 10 – 2 – 4 – 9 – 6 – 3 – 1 – 8

KV 12 Speech acts in communication

1 Possible order: 9 – 5 – 1/2/3/4 – 6/7/8 – 10
2 7, 5, 3, 8, 4, 10, 6, 9, 2, 1

KV 17 Spoken language – everyday English

1

	formal	**informal**
Agreeing	I entirely agree. I suppose some people might see it like that.	I'm totally with you there. You hit the nail on the head. Well, not a bad idea. Fine with me.
Disagreeing	I wonder if we shouldn't ... I have to contradict you there. That doesn't seem convincing to me. I find that hard to believe.	Nonsense! You must be joking. I can't believe you said that. No way. You what?
Admitting that you are wrong	I have to apologize, I didn't take that into account.	I'm so stupid. I was totally wrong. Sorry, I can sometimes be such an idiot.

KV 19 Speaking in test situations

1 Independent monologue: 1, 4, 6; guided monologue: 4, 6; teacher / exam panel dialogue: 4, 5, 7; equal partners dialogue: 2, 3, 4, 5, 7
2 1 d, 2 e, 3 a, 4 c, 5 g, 6 h, 7 f, 8 b

Texte und Abbildungen – KV 1, Seite 1: Volkhard Binder, Berlin; **Seite 2:** Volkhard Binder, Berlin; Dan Reynolds/www.CartoonStock.com; **Seite 3:** Aufgaben 4 a) und b) basieren auf Penny Ur/Andrew Wright, *Five-Minute Activities* (Cambridge University Press 1992), S. 73–74 und S. 90–92; © ddpimages/AP/Manish Swarup; **KV 4:** Barack Obama, Rede zum Wahlsieg, 5.11.08; **KV 5:** Anja Bergler, „Der traditionelle Almabtrieb in den bayerischen Alpen“: www.bayern-blogger.de/2010/09/09; **KV 8:** „Herzlich willkommen in der Frauenkirche“: www.frauenkirche-dresden.de; **KV 15:** Aufgabe 1 basiert auf Friederike Klippel, *Keep talking: Communicative Fluency Activities for Language Teaching* (Cambridge University Press, 1985), S. 29–30; „Design for Fashion Label, New York City“: © http://www.praktika. de/auslandspraktikum-internship/internscout/design-fashion-label-new-york-city-56816.html

Speaking

Teaching SKILLS

Verfasserin: Dr. Annette Leithner-Brauns, Dresden

Verlagsredaktion: Dr. Christian v. Raumer

Design und technische Umsetzung: MatMil Translations & Desktop Publishing, Berlin

Umschlaggestaltung: sans serif, Berlin

www.cornelsen.de

Die Links zu externen Webseiten Dritter, die in diesem Lehrwerk angegeben sind, wurden vor Drucklegung sorgfältig auf ihre Aktualität geprüft. Der Verlag übernimmt keine Gewähr für die Aktualität und den Inhalt dieser Seiten oder solcher, die mit ihnen verlinkt sind.

1. Auflage, 1. Druck 2012

Druck: H. Heenemann, Berlin

ISBN 978-3-06-033009-6

Inhalt gedruckt auf säurefreiem Papier aus nachhaltiger Forstwirtschaft.